KUSTOM PAINTING SECRETS

by Jon Kosmoski

Published by:
Wolfgang Inc.
13895 - 236th St.
Scandia, MN 55073

First published in 1995 by Wolfgang Publications Inc., 13895 236th
St. No., Scandia, MN 55073, USA.

© Timothy Remus - All photos with exception of product and archival.
© Jon Kosmoski - All text.

ISBN number: 0-9641358-3-3

Printed and bound in the USA

On the Cover:

Owned by Billy Gibbons of ZZ TOP © fame, CadZZilla © uses
House of Kolor candy eggplant paint over a grey base to enhance
the unique body lines.

Owned and built by Dave Perewitz with help from brother Donnie
and Russ Keene, the wild Harley-Davidson is painted in a single
stage red. The flames were done with Shimrin basecoats and then
everything was buried in multiple clearcoats - all paints from the
House of Kolor.

Kustom Painting Secrets

Contents

Introduction 5

Chapter One
 History 6

Chapter Two
 How to Set Up a Shop 12

Special Section
 Color Painting Sequences 33

Chapter Three
 Preparation for Paint 41

Chapter Four
 Final Paint Application 60

Chapter Five
 In the Shop: Basic Paint Jobs 80

Chapter Six
 In the Shop: Beyond Basic Paint 98

Chapter Seven
 In the Shop: Custom Paint Jobs 114
 Sources 128

From the Publisher

Jon Kosmoski was already a legend by the time I started reading "car" magazines like *Hot Rod* and *Rod & Custom* in the early 1960s. I remember riding my bike down 28th Street in Minneapolis when my buddy Ron pointed out that, "Jon Kosmoski's shop is just down the street over there." Custom cars and hot rods were really cool and Jon was one of the people who created those neat cars we yearned to own - the cars we read about in the magazines.

Little did I know that thirty-some years later I would be the man helping Jon Kosmoski assemble and publish the fourth edition Kustom Painting Secrets.

I was impressed with Jon before I knew him, I'm even more impressed after spending the last six months trying to keep up with him. Jon is a hands-on guy who likes to do everything himself. I'm pleased to be the person he chose to publish this fourth edition.

In closing I would like to thank Jon and Pat Kosmoski, and all the staff at House of Kolor, for their help in putting this book together.

Timothy Remus

Introduction

Thirty years of techniques & tricks

What is custom painting? Custom painting is an attitude, with a commitment to quality and pride in workmanship. You must want to do it right and take the time to fully understand the methods, equipment and products. Custom painting, once mastered, is an art form as much as any other creative endeavor.

I want you to apply the best paint job possible. And with a basic knowledge of painting and by carefully following our instructions you can apply a quality custom paint job the first time. It would be difficult to cover every aspect of custom painting in this manual, but I will reveal trade secrets that were hard earned so that you can avoid costly mistakes.

In all my years as a painter I have always enjoyed making vehicles look better than new. I've won well over 100 best paint awards and a body shop achievement award for painting 19 cars in a single show. It hasn't always gone smoothly, however, custom painting can be complicated. You must have a total understanding of the products you are using, from primers to klear, and of the equipment used to apply those products.

Our House of Kolor paints are among the best in the world, manufactured at our plant from the best materials money can buy. But the only way to get all that you can from our products is to understand our paints and follow the directions for each product. Mixing ratios, time-between-coats and application guidelines must be totally understood and followed or failure is very probable. The key to a successful paint job is you - your

attitude and your ability to correctly use each product.

Once accomplished, custom painting puts you above standard painters who have not taken the time or interest to study this exciting segment of the refinishing trade. The rewards are there, the pride of doing what only a select few painters across the country have achieved. So now it's up to you to use this book and our House of Kolor paints to produce the best paint jobs in the world.

Chapter One

History

Where I'm coming from

THE EARLY YEARS

My interest in cars and motorcycles started early, back in my high school days in Minneapolis, Minnesota where I grew up. My brother, Jim, shared my fascination with mechanical things and

when I was about sixteen years old we went together to buy a set of torches. That really got us started working on cars.

In high school I always got bored, it was like, "get me to the meat and potatoes of the thing." I

My first car, the 1940 Chevy. It was someone else's failed paint job on this car that pushed me to repaint the car -

and start me off on a whole new career as a custom painter and eventually a paint manufacturer.

This three window coupe was another of my early cars. My friends remember it as being very straight and very, very black.

first compressor was tiny, probably not even one horsepower. It was always: paint for two minutes, wait five for the compressor to catch up, then paint for another two or three.

As soon as I got out of high school Dad co-signed a loan so I could buy my first bike, a 58 BSA Golden Flash. You had to be your own mechanic in those days and I learned a lot just keeping the bike running. We took the bikes out to California in 1960, which

was like the other kids, with a *Hot Rod* or *Rod & Custom* magazine inside the school book so it looked from the front of the room like I was studying algebra.

At first I was more involved in mechanics than in painting or body work. I was always tuning up my own cars or my friend's cars and adjusting the valves and that sort of thing. During high school I worked part time at a gas station and when I graduated I started working full time as an apprentice mechanic.

People ask what got me started painting and really it was my first car, the 1940 Chevy. After I'd had the Chevy for a while I wanted a cool paint job so I took it to this guy in town, the one everyone said was the best painter. He painted it but it wasn't any good. When I went to buff it out there were onion rings in the paint and the whole job wasn't very good.

And I thought, 'he's the best huh?' So I took a night class at Dunwoody Industrial Institute, it was *Body Work and Painting.* And then I started doing more and more body and paint work. I was painting motorcycles in my Mom's basement, but with the paint fumes that didn't last too long. My

My office seems to get more and more cluttered. Old trophies on the shelf, a million magazines on the desk and the floor full of parts for my next motorcycle project.

was quite a trip. Of course we went to Los Angeles and met George Barris and walked through his shop. He treated us great and we are friends to this day. That was a pretty neat trip, I remember being very impressed with the paint jobs I saw, not just at the Barris shop but on the street too.

FIRST PAINT JOBS

After high school when I was still working as a mechanic, I would take my paycheck and go down and blow it at the paint supply

I like to have full control of the manufacturing process. We even make our own color chip charts with the strange looking machine you see here.

store. Then I would try to create my own unique colors. I painted my friend's cars and things like that. I was already buying my own pearl materials and mixing my own unique colors.

We were doing tri-coat paint jobs (basecoat, candy or pearl, and then a clearcoat) even back then. I was one of the first in Minnesota to do a candy job. In fact, I used to make my own candies by taking nitrocellulose lacquer toners and mixing them with pigments. In those days all the paints were either nitrocellulose lacquers or alkyd enamels. For custom painting everyone used the lacquers but there were some problems. The sun would fade the colors in a short time and sometimes the base color would discolor so then the job was ruined. Cold cracking was a problem too because the nitrocellulose became brittle with age, especially when we put ten or more coats on a car. That early paint couldn't flex as the temperature changed so it would crack in cold weather.

Acrylic lacquers were introduced in the late 1950s to overcome the problems inherent with the nitro based lacquers. And it was the change over to the new material that really got me to start manufacturing my own paints.

We are a true paint manufacturer. We grind all our own pigments and mix our own paints in house.

THE FIRST KUSTOM PAINTS

When the new acrylic lacquer paints came out I thought, "Wow, this will be great." They said the new paints wouldn't crack like the nitrocellulose materials did so I went down to the paint store and bought a pint of each one of their toners. When I got back to the shop and looked at the actual color of the new acrylic lacquer toners I thought, 'this is garbage.' That's when I decided to try and make or mix my own acrylic lacquer paint. My idea was to combine the color of the old nitro lacquers with the durability of the new acrylic materials. I figured that if I could do that I'd really have something. And it was that idea that really pushed me off into paint manufacturing.

I used to experiment a lot late at night and one night I really hit it, I got some great colors. About the same time my wife Pat took an art class at night and she met this fella who was a polymer chemist. He was designing resins for General Mills, a real bright guy but he didn't understand custom paints. When I told him what I was trying to do and some of the problems I was having he gave me names of other chemists who were in a better position to answer my questions. That's when it really started. Those chemists were able to answer most of my questions about paint or at least give me hints and tell me which books to read. For awhile

It's hard to believe that we started out selling an occasional quart can of a special lacquer mix to friends at the car shows. Today our line incudes our patented Shimrin basecoats which can be topcoated with our lacquer or urethane based kandys and clearcoats.

I've enjoyed motorcycles from the time I was a kid. This is my first Harley-Davidson, a customized Shovelhead.

I was in the library all the time.

When I started making paint I had some failures. I learned everything the hard way but I did learn. I was buying raw materials from the big supply houses so sometimes I could get help from the manufacturers. As time went on I got so I could mix better and better colors. Because I was manufacturing my own paints and mixing my own colors, I could produce better paint jobs than the other

Not my last, but certainly one of my latest Harley-Davidsons.

At House of Kolor we have technicians ready to answer your questions - just dial (612) 729-1044 and ask for "technical."

shops. The quality of the paint jobs meant more and more trophies at the various car shows. My early reputation was based on my candy jobs. My paint jobs almost always won Best Paint at the car show. Pretty soon guys would come to me at the show, compliment the paint and then ask, "Can I buy a quart of that paint for my next project?"

HOUSE OF KOLOR IS BORN

One day I called a printer and asked him about making labels for my paint cans. Of course I needed a name. We started calling the body shop House of Color in 1959 and then George Barris was spelling Kustom with a K and my last name starts with a K so we changed 'color' to 'kolor' and that was the name we put on the new paint cans - it seemed like a natural. We've been manufacturing and selling our own paints since 1965. We started out with acrylic lacquers, which we called Kustom Kolor, but pretty soon I wanted to add urethane to our line of paint products. I did my first urethane job in 1971 but it wasn't until a little later that I found a European urethane system that I liked. That's when we began manufacturing urethanes under the name Kosmic Kolor. Eventually we registered most of our trade names, both in this country and other countries too.

MY FIRST SHOP

It was a few years after high school that I opened my first shop. Actually I went into partnership with a well known pinstriper in town, Frank Nickolas. We called ourselves Nickolas and Kosmoski Painters. We rented some space from a small body shop but the partnership didn't last very long. About the time the partnership came apart the guy we were renting space from decided to sell out. So I agreed to rent the whole shop and buy out his equipment.

At that time I already had a family so I kept the regular job as a mechanic and would work at my own shop at night. I had a guy in there working during the day and then at night I would come in and help finish up the work. That went on for a number of years until I figured we had enough work that I could quit the day job and just concentrate on the body shop. That was in the early 1960s and I've been at it ever since. Once I was in the shop full time I had more time to experiment with paints and it was about two years later that we started selling paint under our own House of Kolor name.

If there's one reason for my success and a hint that I can pass on to other painters, it's my natural curiosity. Whenever I see a great paint job, I wonder, "How did he do that," or "how could I do it better." You have to have your own flair, your own style and a desire to do the very best work.

THE FUTURE

The new challenges for us include reduced VOCs (volatile organic compounds), not just in California but much of the rest of the country as well. And we've had to find new pigments for some of the paints, pigments that contain no lead. Of course we have some new products like the Marblizers and more on the way. Our new candy basecoat system will allow painters to achieve the look of a candy paint job more easily and with less paint build up. We also have a new Kandy mixing system on the way based on a special mixing clear and super concentrated candy pigments, all designed to reduce inventory. The formulas will be provided for all our Kandy kolors, but anyone with a little creativity will be able to mix their own unique kolors.

For over thirty years I've been trying to provide painters with the brightest, most brilliant paints possible in a system that's easy to use. House of Kolor will continue to buy the best materials money can buy and use them to manufacture the brightest, truest paints available.

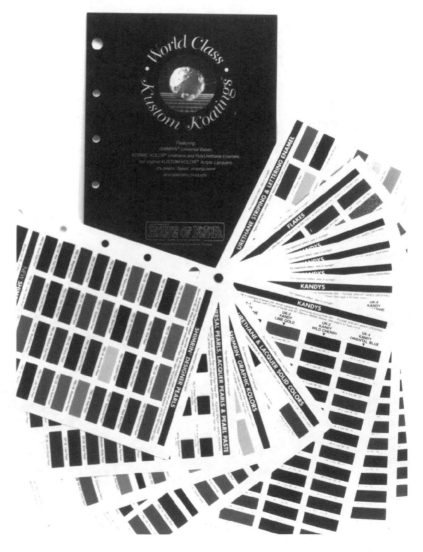

Our new Kustom Koatings paint chip chart has over 12 pages of colorful ideas and over 430 individual paint chips.

Chapter Two

How To Set Up A Shop

And keep it safe and legal

First you need to check your rules and regulations to see if you're allowed to paint in your area. In residential areas it may be prohibitive. Be sure to check your local codes and laws. Whether it be in a shop you're setting up at your home or in a commercial area the rules are pretty much the same. Assuming you are working within local building codes, you need to set up your shop so it's both efficient and safe. Remember though that if you're just doing a one-time paint job most of

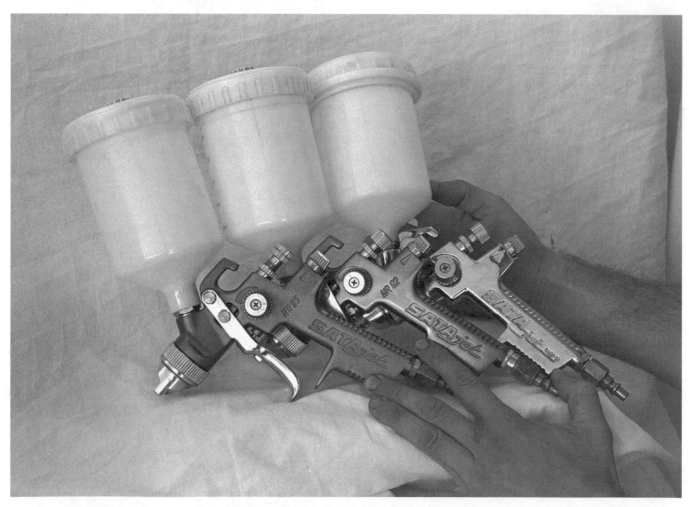

Spray guns come in a wide variety of styles, including gravity feed like these guns from Sata.

the equipment we recommend can be rented.

AIR SUPPLY

For painting I think setting your air system up right is most critical. It doesn't really affect safety but it certainly affects the paint job. You must feed clean dry air to your spray gun.

In a small area you want to go with 3/4 inch feeder lines as the minimum size. It doesn't cost that much more to go to inch and a half, whatever size you use it should be galvanized pipe. Whenever a 3/4 inch feeder line takes off from the main line the fitting should run up and then turn back down so you don't get any moisture or oil in the line to the spray gun. I get in a few shops now that are using this schedule-eighty plastic stuff. I've already been there and done that. My experience with them was horrible because the system came apart twice in the hottest days of the summer under hard use. Every corner gets extremely hot. It gets so hot you can't touch it and then the glue lets go and it's like shrapnel when they blow. I had a car all done and ready to paint one time and it got marks all over it from the pipe blowing.

I like to use galvanized pipe and I use Gasoila as a sealer on the fittings. That stuff gets like a paint. After using the Gasoila you shouldn't introduce air into the system until 24 hours after you've done your last fitting. I like to put shut-offs at the regulator and at the main compressor so it's easy if you want to bleed a line or change a fitting on a regulator.

I set up my first air systems the way everybody does, with no shut-offs. Then you get a leaking unit and you have to remember to come in the next morning and take care of it right away before you turn the compressor on. I like to be able to take care of that

Don't skimp when you buy an air compressor. Five horsepower is the minimum but remember you can rent one for that occasional paint job.

You need an area you can keep clean and you need air movement so the paint will dry correctly. I like to paint the walls of the booth with two-part paint and then coat it with a sticky tack material. That way the dust sticks to the walls and when the booth gets dirty you can just power-wash the walls.

A TC23, which is basically a double-charcoal respirator, is a necessity for painting with non-catalyzed paints. You should also wear a TC23 for sanding zinc chromate primers. The good ones have replaceable pre-filters and charcoal filters.

maintenance right now when it's leaking. Every time the compressor starts and stops you have to think of a dollar bill with wings on it.

Some type of a fine micronic filter inside the booth right where you introduce the air to the gun is a great idea. Either right before or after the regulator. I've done mine after the regulator and then I put my fittings on the outlet of the filter. And you need a good water trap of course. It should be located near the regulator instead of being mounted right at the com-

For spraying paints catalyzed with isocyanates you should wear an air-supply hood or mask (a TC19C) supplied air from its own oil-free compressor.

pressor.

For a compressor you need a minimum of five horsepower to keep up with a DA-sander or paint gun for one guy. If you put two people on a DA sander or two painting with production guns a five horse compressor will not keep up. For a bigger shop my advice has always been to buy two fives rather than going into a ten horse compressor. The reason being it costs more but you never have down time if one of the compressors breaks. You've always got a working compressor to keep you in business.

This oil-free compressor is designed to supply an air-supply hood. This model has enough capacity to supply two painters using two masks or hoods.

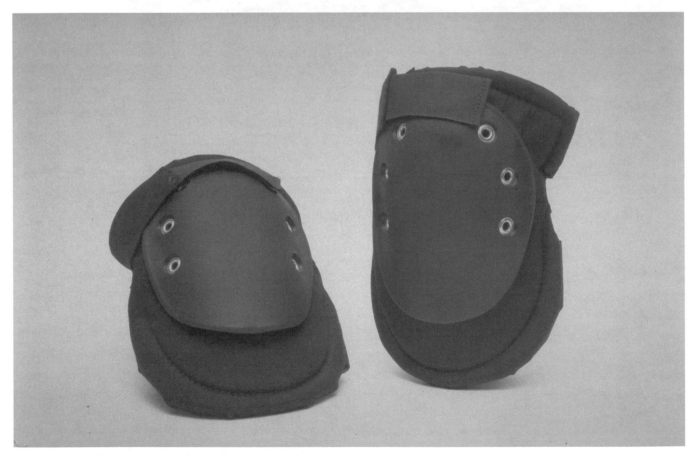

It's not just your lungs you need to worry about. Knee pads like these from Morgan manufacturing will save the carti- *lage in your knees when you have to spend time kneeling on the floor.*

For painting with isocyanate-catalyzed paint you need to wear an air-supply hood, and a complete painter's suit.

You can have one shut off earlier than the other so it's a helper compressor to come in to fill that void when it's needed.

After the compressor has been run 50 hours I like to change the oil with a brand of synthetic reciprocating compressor oil. I have had some people tell me that they think that causes fish eyes. I've used it for too many years for anybody to tell me that. I use Amzoil reciprocating compressor oil, it's made for a regular reciprocating compressor. You'll cut down on maintenance on the com-

These are two of the many guns in the House of Kolor arsenal: A Sharpe HVLP on the left and a high-pressure gun from Sata. Both are siphon feed designs.

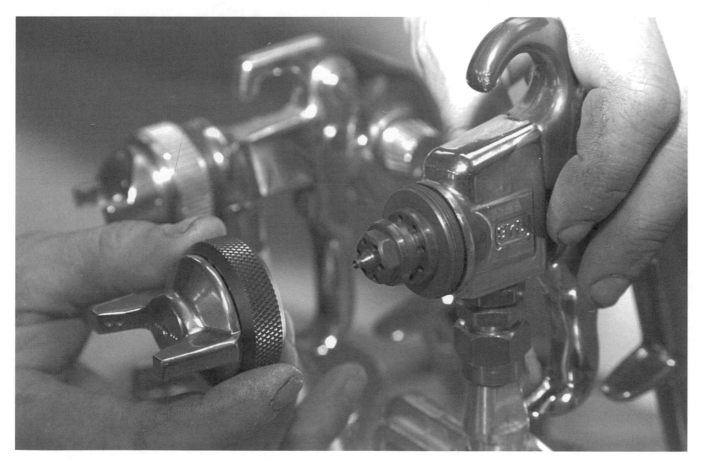

Behind the air cap is the fluid tip and needle. The combination of cap, tip and needle determine how much *paint a particular gun will flow and how much air it will consume.*

Ergonomically designed to fit your hand and spray from nearly any angle, this new OMX gun from DeVilbiss meets all the standards for HVLP.

pressor(s). The valves last longer. All the reciprocating components last longer and the oil, because there is no combustion, never gets dirty. It stays clean as a whistle for years. I just change it for drill once a year.

Also, always use a quality spray type hose either from Binks or DeVilbiss or one of the other quality hose manufacturers because that way you have a hose with a lot of flexibility and one that won't fragment on the inside. Particularly with a touch-up gun, that little hose is a good idea. You don't need a hose that restricts movement when you're really finessing things.

The hose should be 5/16 inch minimum inside diameter. Nobody uses 3/8 inch. I have seen 3/8 and they're clumsy. It's almost overkill. What I tell people at seminars is, 'If your regulator is in the front of the booth, run the hose from the regulator down to the floor, turn and go over to the side of the booth, turn again and go to the end of the booth, then go across the booth and cut the hose. That's where you put your fitting. That gives you just enough hose to go anywhere in that booth and no more. I get a pressure gauge that I snap on the end of the hose. Then I hook up the gun and then I set my regulator for what I think is right. With full trigger pull I look to see what I'm getting for pressure at the gun. With a gauge at the gun you'll see the difference in the pressures between the two areas because there is an automatic pressure drop that takes place in the hose.

By having that gauge to check your pressure each time you paint you are more accurate. Now it's easier to come back and match something or touch something up later because you know exactly what the pressure was. And by filtering

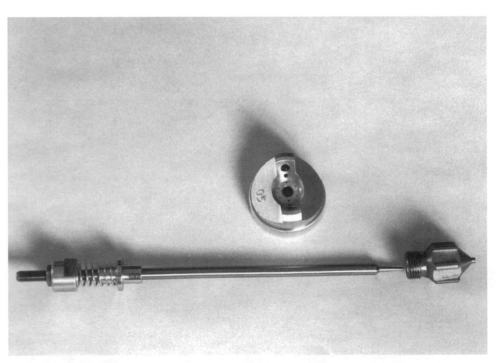

Sometimes called the fluid set, the air cap, fluid tip and needle are most commonly changed as a complete set (check the recommendations of the manufacturer). By changing the fluid set you can spray very different materials with the same gun.

that air with a micron filter and using a good water trap you're sure to feed the gun clean dry air. That air must be filtered and kept dry. You need to pull from the top of the feeder line and that line should run downhill slightly with a clean-out valve at the end. Tricks like that are critical to your survival as a day-to-day painter.

THE BOOTH OR PAINTING AREA

You need air movement in the booth, most good booths move 50 to 100 lineal feet of air per minute. You also need some form of exhaust filters to catch paint before it goes into the atmosphere. There are some companies that make prep stations that will do just that, exhaust the fumes, then pull them through the filter. You need some air movement for the paint to dry properly. That air moving by the object pulls solvent from the paint, without air movement always use the faster reducer. The air movement also makes it a safer environment for you as a painter.

They do make exhaust filters out of a foam type material that can be dissolved in solvent so they can go with your waste solvent. (The filters have to be disposed of properly as hazardous waste.) That's what a lot of people do. If you get the fiberglass style they can be shaken out and used again and again if you want to take the time to do that.

Most booths are required to have a sprinkler system in today's world. But you may not be able to do that. There are some medium cost, dry-charged fire extinguishers that you can set up in a small shop so that you could do it that way. I've seen guys make booths out of sheet rock in a small shop. If you paint your booth, put a two-part catalyzed paint on it and let it harden and then come in and put the water-borne spray-away material over

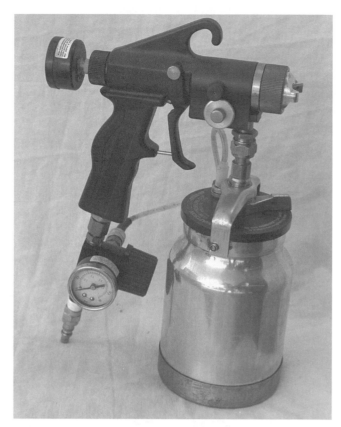

This HVLP gun from Mattson offers a gauge on the back of the handle to directly measure pressure at the air cap (most HVLP designs stay under 10 psi at the cap). The Mattson gun allows the user to adjust the pressure on the paint in the pot - as monitored by the second gauge.

Most air caps have a series of ports or holes, in addition to the center hole. The extra ports provide additional air for improved atomization and, in the case of the ports in the "horns," shape the fan.

Different Types of Spray Guns

Choosing a spray gun used to be a relatively simple matter of matching your budget to the available guns at the local parts store. Once purchased, it was just a matter of learning to use the gun and keeping it clean. Yet, the world of spray painting and spray painting guns has changed dramatically in the last few years.

Today there is more than one type of spray gun. The standard siphon (or high-pressure gun) has been joined by the newer HVLP gun (high volume low pressure). Both types are available with pressure pots, gravity feed cups and remote paint reservoirs.

HIGH-PRESSURE SIPHON-STYLE GUNS

The high pressure siphon type paint gun was invented by a man named DeVilbiss and used during the Civil War to spray and atomize medicines and disinfectants. The new guns manufactured by companies like DeVilbiss, Binks, Sharpe and a dozen more are far superior to anything Mr. DeVilbiss conceived during the war, yet they owe their basic design to that early pioneer.

The high pressure guns are known for good atomization. The high speed air stream (usually forty psi or more) does a good job of breaking up the paint and delivering it to the object being painted. On the other hand, that high speed air stream moves the paint at high speed toward - but not always onto - the object being sprayed. Some of the paint misses the object entirely, some of it hits with such force that it bounces back off into the air. Standard siphon style guns get as little as 25 percent of the paint on the car. The rest of the paint, as well as the solvents mixed with the paint, go up in the air or out with the exhaust.

The paint industry has a means of measuring the amount of material that actually goes on the object. Transfer efficiency (or TE) is simply a measure of the amount of paint that actually makes it from the gun to the object. Siphon style guns commonly have a transfer efficiency of only about 25 percent. The new HVLP guns by contrast have efficiencies of 75 percent and more.

HVLP

HVLP stands for high volume low pressure - these guns and systems

Accuspray pressurized (siphon style) spray guns were pioneers in HVLP technology. The gun body is a hi tech composite.

atomize the paint with a high volume of low pressure air instead of the standard high-pressure siphon type gun where a small volume of high pressure air is used to atomize the paint.

By delivering roughly three times as much material to the object the amount of paint used is reduced. This means lower material costs for painting, less overspray in the atmosphere (and on the walls of the shop) and less solvent usage meaning reduced VOCs in the atmosphere. It also means less mist in the paint booth for you to breathe during the painting operation.

Though there are HVLP guns that run off their own small turbine, most guns used to spray automotive-type finishes are compressor driven. These guns are able to convert the high pressure compressor air to a low pressure air - with more volume - inside the gun. The air leaving the gun measures less than ten psi. Some siphon guns pressurize the paint in the pot and use that pressure to bring the paint up to meet the air stream.

HVLP guns tend to cost more than comparable high-pressure siphon guns. The HVLP equipment makes more sense when you consider the fact that an HVLP system will use less paint and create less overspray. Most HVLP systems will create less than half the overspray meaning less chance to breathe the often toxic fumes and less clean up in the shop afterwards. The better examples make candy painting easier due to their uniform fine atomization of the paint.

SPRAY GUN ANATOMY
HIGH-PRESSURE SIPHON-TYPE GUNS

The modern high-pressure, siphon-type guns from Binks, DeVilbiss, Sharpe, Sata and all the others feature the same basic design. Essentially, air passing through the spray gun siphons paint from the pot, or can that is usually incorporated into the design of the gun. The two-stage trigger controls both air and liquid - pulling the trigger back part way allows air to pass through the gun while pulling it back all the way allows liquid paint to be pulled from the cup. That liquid paint is introduced into the air stream at the point where the air leaves the gun.

Paint and air both leave the gun at the air cap and immediately begin to mix. Atomization occurs in two or three stages, beginning when the fluid leaves the gun, surrounded by a column of air that leaves the gun from the ring surrounding the fluid nozzle tip. Most air caps have at least one more set of air

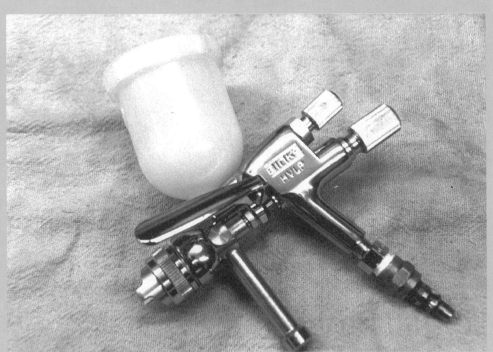

You don't have to buy a big gun to enjoy the advantages of HVLP. This Binks touch up gun is a full HVLP design and uses a gravity feed cup.

ports near the fluid nozzle tip that provide additional air to the paint and air mixture as it leaves the gun. These additional ports provide secondary atomization. Most guns have small air ports in the "horns" of the air cap. These are used primarily to shape the paint fan though the additional air serves to aid atomization of the paint as well.

Most spray guns of the type we describe have two basic adjustments, the two small knobs commonly seen on the back of the gun. The top knob controls air to the horns of the air cap and thus is used to control the size of the fan. The lower knob controls the material or the amount of fluid leaving the gun.

Before adjusting the gun to spray a nice pattern you need to buy the right air cap and fluid nozzle. Different materials require the

use of different air caps and fluid nozzles, and each set has a different CFM rating. Be sure to match the cap and fluid nozzle to both the material you are spraying and the capacity of your compressor. If your compressor size is limited then a larger one can be rented when you're ready to do that paint job.

When it comes to setting the adjustments on a new high-pressure gun we like to use the gun with the top adjustment wide open and the material knob backed out enough to give the pattern size required for the object being painted.

There are a few basic points to keep in mind when you use that new spray gun: Try to follow the pressure recommendations you find in our tech sheets (available for free just by calling us). Ultimately, the correct pressure is

It is the amount of air passing through the ports on the outside of the air cap (the "horns") that determines the shape of the paint fan.

the one that gives you the pattern you want. One more thing, gun manufacturer's (both high-pressure and HVLP) report that nearly all the complaints they receive can be traced to dirty equipment - so always keep the equipment clean.

HVLP GUNS

HVLP guns are very similar to the high-pressure siphon guns in their basic anatomy. A one or two-stage trigger controls fluid and air flow.

Though the new HVLP guns aren't nearly as "universal" in their adjustments as the old high-pressure siphon-style guns they all have two basic adjustments, material and fan shape, though not always in the location of the traditional high-pressure guns. Some allow the painter to adjust the amount of pressure on the paint in the pot.

As is the case with high-pressure guns, the first step with your new HVLP system is to install the right air cap and fluid nozzle for the material at hand. If you're converting to an HVLP after years of using siphon-style guns, remember that these guns transfer more material to the object, so adjust the gun and paint accordingly.

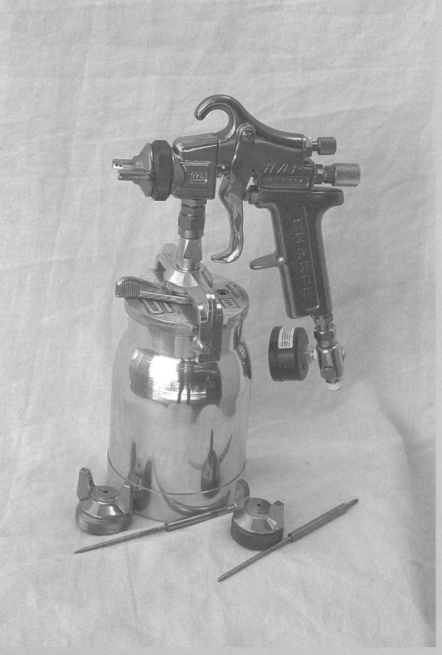

By changing air caps, needles and often the fluid tip (not shown), one spray gun will display very different characteristics in terms of the c.f.m. requirements, pattern size and the amount of material applied.

A touch up gun is a nice addition to your tool supply, especially if you do custom work, graphics and flames.

that. I like the stuff that doesn't dry, because it holds the lint and the dirt that gets airborne in the booth. It makes the whole booth a tack area. Some people don't like that because they lean against the booth and it gets all over them.

SHOP SAFETY

You need different levels of protection for different situations. For sanding and grinding you should wear a particle filter and a good pair of safety glasses. 3M is now making particle masks with charcoal in them, they're nice and offer protection from more than just dust. Be sure to wear safety glasses whenever you're grinding. I prefer the safety glasses that fit tight to your face when you're grinding on steel for doing body work. I have tried all the other style of safety glasses and have managed to still get metal in my eye with those types. I like the tight fitting ones for that reason.

For non-catalyzed painting situations you need a TC23, which is basically a double-charcoal respirator. Be sure to replace both the pre-filters and the charcoal canisters as recommended by the manufacturer - you've only got one set of lungs and you must protect them at all times. By the way, when you dry sand our epoxy zinc chromate primer (our EP-2 and KP-2), you need to wear a TC23 respirator (not just a particle mask) because of the zinc chromate (by the time you

Extra paint cups for the touch up gun mean you can mix all your colors before you come into the booth which makes the whole job go much faster. It's always a good idea to carefully check and adjust the spray pattern before you start painting.

read this we will have a new chromate-free, hi-solid, bleed-resistant epoxy primer that survives over 1000 hours in our salt-spray heated test cabinet).

For painting with isocyanates - the top coats, mainly that's when you're going to need protection - you need to use a TC19C, which is an air supply hood. The prices of those are coming down. The people making them are making them more efficiently. Although they do have some filters now that allow you to breathe reciprocating compressor air, most times you can't because of the fact that it has oil particles in it which cause pneumonia for anyone who breathes them.

For the air supply to one of these hoods they generally use a small, oil-less compressor constantly feeding air into your mask. It's pressurized and you're constantly expelling the contaminated air that you're exhausting. That is becoming a very important part of the spray operation. Anybody that has a commercial shop on the street can't run the risk of a lawsuit by not having that. We have one that's a dual unit for teaching. Two people can get hooked up on it. It's got the option of the full face or just a mask covering the nose and mouth. The nice thing about the full face is that it does cover more skin. The disadvantage of it is that when you're spraying it hazes the mask so you have to put some "tear-aways" on and they make them. So periodically you can tear it away so you get a recleaned view.

You also must wear a respirator when pouring the paints that are catalyzed with isocyanates, because when its a free monomer (before it's mixed) is one of its most hazardous times. Once it's mixed into the paint it becomes less harmful because it's encapsulated.

Paint gun manufacturers send us guns to evaluate - this is just one of our cabinets. To start you need just one gun, but buy a good one. I do think it's a good idea to have two, however, with one dedicated to primer use.

The primer gun will have a large fluid tip orifice, designed to move heavy materials - so it makes a good gun to use when you're shooting metal flake.

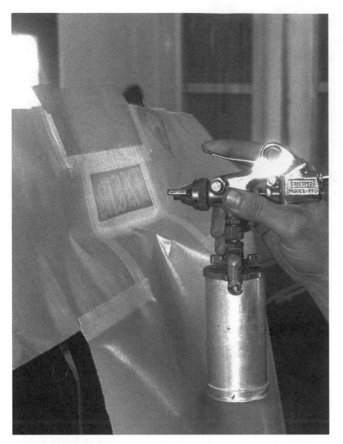

The touch up gun is useful for small jobs like this - painting the signs on the dragster seen later in the book.

A painter's suit is a good idea even when you're painting non-catalyzed paints like our basecoats. The suit keeps the lint on your clothing out of the paint finish.

It's dangerous again when it becomes airborne and you're breathing it and getting it into your system.

PROTECT YOUR BODY

You need a good painter's suit particularly if you're working with anything that's catalyzed on the urethane side. The suit will also prevent lint on your clothes from falling into the paint. Whenever you're putting an isocyanate style catalyst in paint, which is normally used in the acrylic urethanes or the polyurethane's, then you've got to be concerned about air movement and skin contact. One of the major places the toxic fumes enters you body is through the mucous membranes around your eyes. So if the mask doesn't cover your eyes you need goggles or safely glasses that fit tight around the eyes.

When you're spraying, get out of the room between coats. Set up a timing system. There's no point to stay in the room between coats. You need some form of exhaust system to expel the fumes safely and trap the over spray.

The epoxy paints are not as bad. They're catalyzed with a polyamade and it's less hazardous than the isocyanates. Obviously you want to wear a TC23 respirator when you're spraying or mixing these materials but you don't need the separate air supply for that material.

GLOVES.

Your skin is receptive and porous so you shouldn't get your hands into these materials, it's another good reason to wear gloves and a protective suit. Some experts claim that the doctor's examining gloves are not as effective as they should be because there is some porosity. A better glove is the 100 percent Nitrile gloves, they handle the solvents perfectly. These are available as a throw away but they're kind of expensive.

400 units of Vitamin E, taken every day, is a good preventive measure. The vitamin E takes the free radicals that might get in your system from the isocyanates and puts them in the body's waste chain so they don't get lodged in your organs.

REMEMBER YOUR KNEES

We have to protect your knees from kneeling on concrete for extended periods of time, it will damage those joints. Extended kneeling on the concrete will ruin the cartilage. I've done it, I already know. This is very, very important

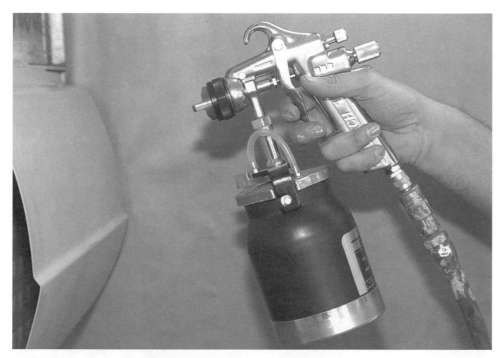

When spraying you need to keep the gun 90 degrees to the surface being painted.

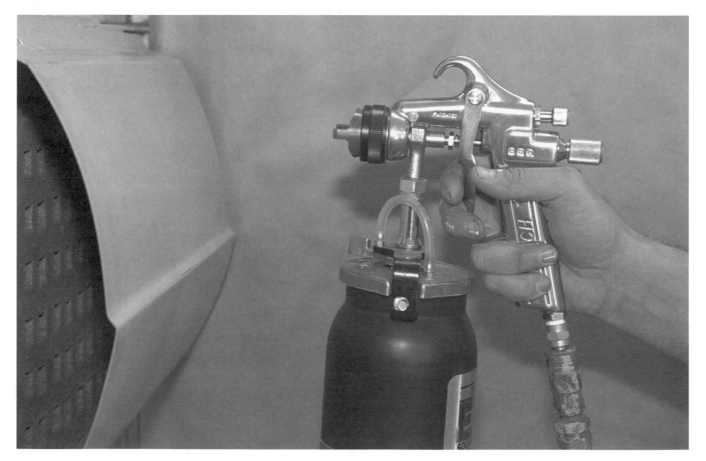

Failure to keep the gun 90 degrees to the surface means that one side of the fan will be closer to the surface. Coverage will be uneven and runs may result.

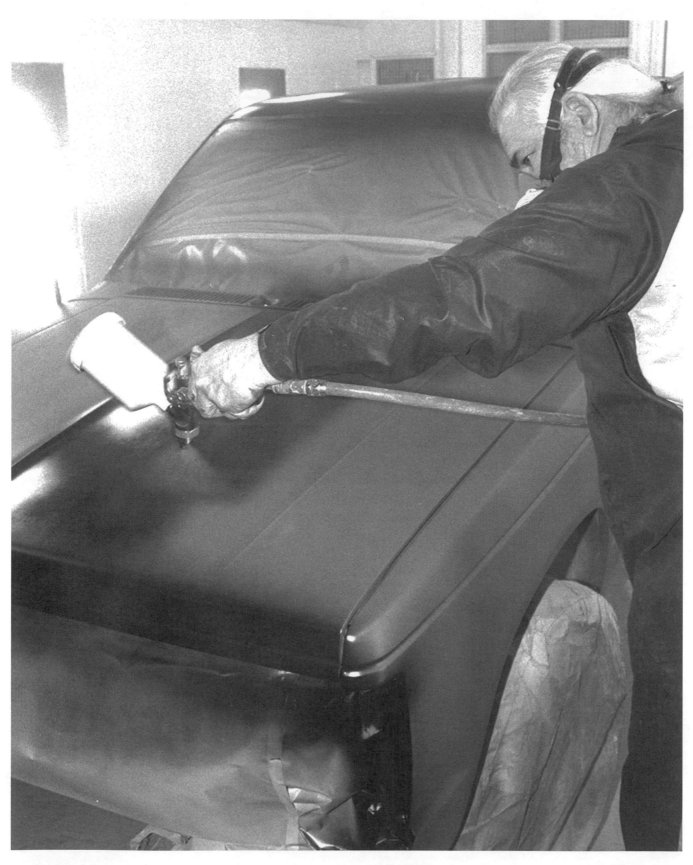

Technique, technique, technique. You have to keep the application even, overlap each pass according to the tech sheet (50 percent in this case) and the gun at 90 degrees to the surface.

fumes in the air so there is less for you to breathe. There are certain objects however that are hard to paint with HVLP, they just don't have the air to push the paint into certain areas.

I really believe that you need to spend money on a primer gun. There are gravity and siphon feed guns specifically set up to move the heavy primers. Nine times out of ten, the gun that you use for primer will also work for metal flake, because the orifice size for that primer gun is in the .080 to .090 inch range. I really prefer a siphon feed type of gun for metal flake because with the gravity-feed gun, when you set it down, the flake settles at the bottom and plugs up the gun.

> **He was unbolting the gas tank and the fumes traveled over to the ignition source, and "boom" before you knew it there was an explosion.**

When you buy the regular gun, (for non-primer use) get some extra needle-air cap sizes for that gun. That way you have some options for working with different materials with different percentage-of-solids content. Accuspray, for example, just came out with another soft spray nozzle for the high solids. So they're all moving toward the high solid equipment to change the way things work.

For custom work you need a touch-up gun for doing the graphic work. It isn't mandatory if you're just starting out, because I worked for many years without one. But for doing your finest work and being in control - by not putting on as much material - a touch up

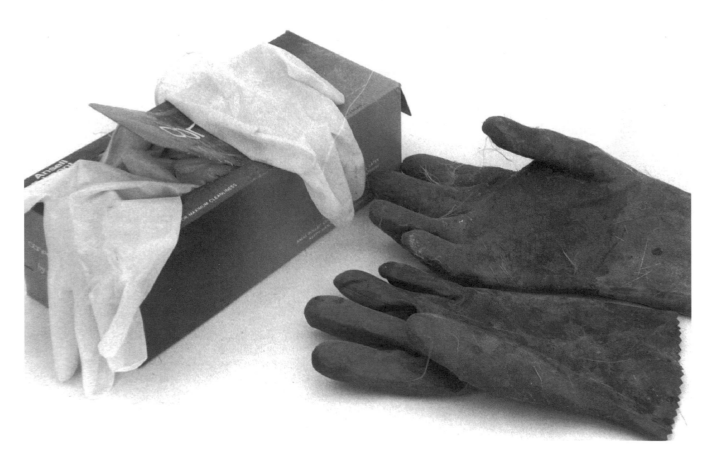

Wear gloves when you're spraying or handling paints, especially the catalyzed paints.

gun works well. There are inexpensive versions out there from Sharp and from some of the overseas manufacturers. If you're a hobby painter it may be all you need to start out. The components are cheap to replace and the guns work very well.

Whenever I get a new hose it goes in the booth and I retire the booth hose for use in the other areas because they do take a lot of wear. I think if you paint everyday, you might replace the hose a couple of times a year. I try not to step on the hose when I'm in the booth or trip up on it because if you're using a pressure pot it turns your pressure pot into a squirt gun. In order to keep the hose from getting caught under the tires there are wedges available that fit in front of the tires. Or you can do it my way with a gallon can full of shot placed in front of the tires. Or you can make something out of tubing. The point is, unless you do something the hose will get stuck underneath the tire where it meets the floor.

CONCLUSION

When you set up your shop buy the best equipment you can afford. All that stuff costs a lot of money so once you own the tools take care of them. Change the oil on the compressor and keep the gun clean. People get in a hurry and they skip

the important things, like the fire extinguishers and the safety equipment and taking the time to put on a respirator when they paint - but when you think about it, what can be more important than your health?

A touch-up gun is very handy for painting small objects like this bicycle frame we did as a promotion for one of the paint industry shows.

PAINTING SEQUENCES

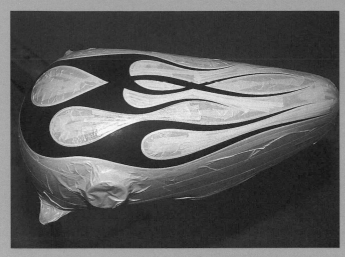

A good flame job starts with a great layout. If you doubt your own ability, hire someone good, a pinstripe and airbrush artist perhaps. This particular layout was done by Kevin Winter.

After taping off parts of the flame licks the darker highlights and shadows are added in cobalt blue to create the impression that one lick goes over or under another.

Three medium coats of BC-02 orion silver form the base for the kandy. The back of the flames are done with four coats of kandy violet KK-17 (mixed with Kandy Koncentrates and SG-100).

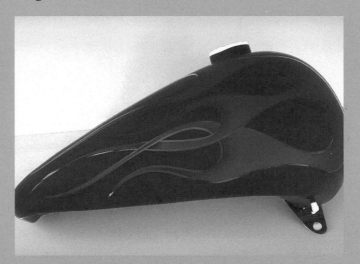

Here's the tank after the tape is pulled and the pinstripes have been added, but before final clearcoat.

Like the violet, the oriental blue, KK-4, is mixed from Koncentrates and applied in four coats. (It's always a good idea to check the color against the color charts as you spray). In order to avoid having the color meet in an abrupt line each successive coat of the second color is brought a little farther into the first color.

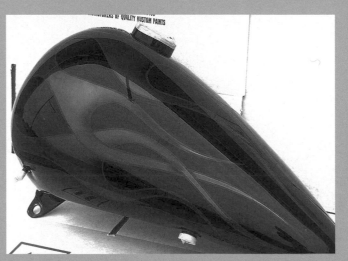

In order to bury the pinstripes we used four coats of UC-1 clear (one tack and three wet) before wet sanding with 500 grit. The final clearcoat is UFC-1, a very high gloss, flexible clear, polished to an even higher luster.

33

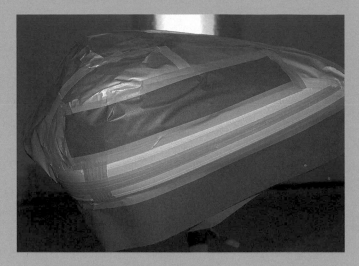

After applying the white basecoat (BC-26) to all the areas that make up the graphics, everything but the two horizontal stripes is taped off.

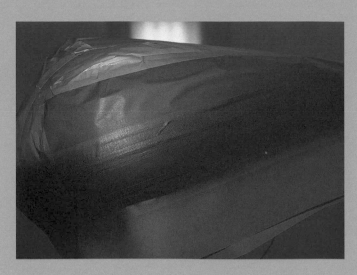

The center stripe is done with two coats of PBC 35 pink pearl fogged with hot pink pearl number PBC-39.

All these colors are our Shimrin Designer Pearls, the bottom stripe is done in PBC 30 sunrise pearl. The upper stripe is PBC-32 tangelo, some tangelo overspray darkens the yellow on the lower stripe.

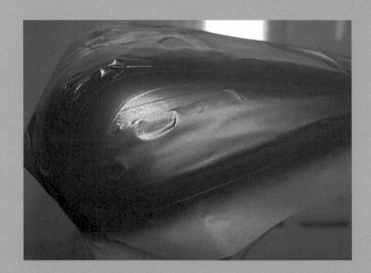

After another round of reverse taping we apply 3 coats of PBC- 65 passion pearl highlighted with PBC 40 violet pearl

Here we have pulled the tape for the center stripe. This is a case where you need to decide what you want for the final design and then work it all backwards so you can do the tape-outs with minimal hussle and no duplication of your work.

The "after" photo. After pinstriping, clearcoating, color sanding and applying three wet final clearcoats with UFC-1.

This is the engine seen in chapter 7. The polished fins and glossy black paint job give the engine a nice look. To get kandy gold over the factory air cleaner and logo we first sprayed it with AP-01 adhesive promoter and then came in with the kandy pagan gold.

We did more than just the engine paint for Mike Marquart's Dyna Low Rider. The sheet metal is painted kandy pagan gold over a silver basecoat, with flames in black and another set of pinstripe flames.

Here you can see the basic design of our logo, in white basecoat surrounded by black with a Marblized rim.

Painting the logo requires a large measure of patience and some careful work with the touch-up gun.

All the logo colors are applied with Kandy Koncentrates mixed in SG-100 for faster coverage.

More than halfway through the logo project, with some very intricate design work still to do.

Because we're using kandies to paint the logo colors, a little overspray on the black won't show.

Here we get ready to paint the third color on the wings.

The Egyptian scarab beetle rolled its food into a ball, suggesting to the ancient Egyptians the rolling of the sun across the sky. Thus the scarab became the symbol of the sun-god. The beetle lived underground and was believed to be reborn every day at noon. It became the symbol of resurrection and eternal life.

Note the dots of color on the upper wings.

We at House of Kolor, Inc. chose the scarab as our company logo because who would show our paint better than the sun-god, especially one with eternal life depicting the long life of our finishes.

Jon K.

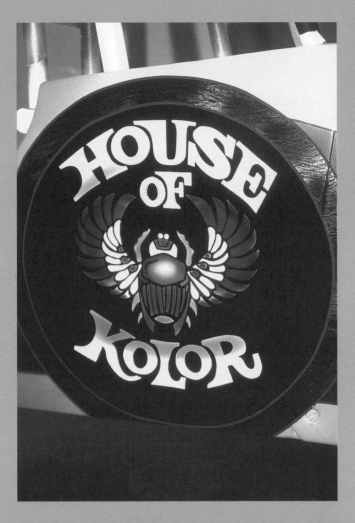

Our company logo and symbol of the sun is looking very bright indeed.

The finished draster, bound to win plenty of trophies for best E.T. and best paint too.

This close up shows the tank with the multi-colored graphics done in Shimrin Designer Pearls.

Here we see Patty Crandall's Sportster from chapter 6. The kandy oriental blue was put down over a blue metallic base before adding the graphics. The painted and polished wheels add a nice touch.

Chapter Three

Preparation For Paint

Things to consider before you start

Ideally, in order to get longevity on a custom paint job, we feel that it should be the only paint job on the vehicle. A custom paint job is a high mil paint job, 10 mils thick or more (each mil is .001 inch thick). There should be a good two-part primer underneath the paint so there's no shrinkage or movement of the primer. What this means is either a chemical or mechanical removal of the existing paint. Particularly if a vehicle has been painted again, other than factory, we highly

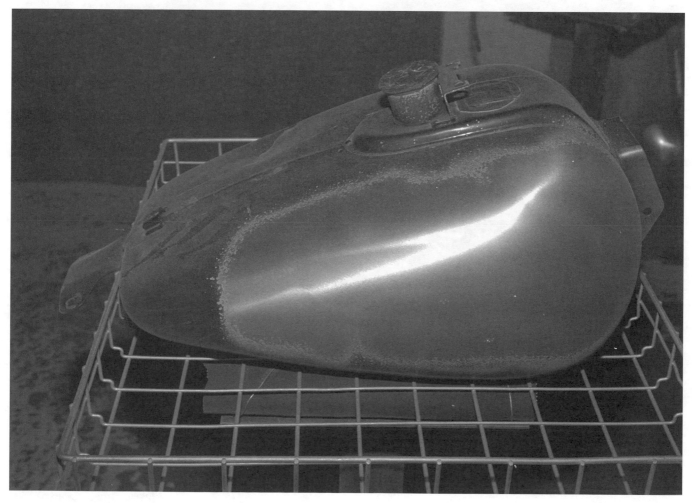

Here a motorcycle tank has been about half stripped - in less than ten minutes. How it takes to get off the paint is determined by the size of the object, and the thickness and condition of the paint.

The blasting booth is like an oversize paint booth and after each session the plastic media is swept into the hopper and used over again.

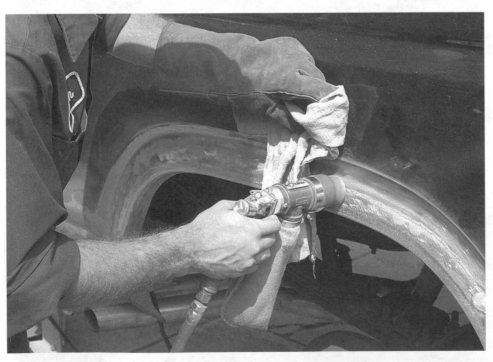

Though large commercial sand blasters can do considerable damage to your sheet metal, small blasters like this little "spot" unit are very handy for eliminating rust in small areas.

recommend that the paint be removed. If it's got factory paint, and you can guarantee that by going around the vehicle with a mil-thickness gauge to guarantee that millage is accurate, then you may be able to paint over that paint.

Generally on the new cars you see the thickness at around three to four mils. If it's much more than that, particularly six to eight mils, you know that either it's gone through the line twice, or it's been painted again probably because of shipping damage or something happened to it at some other point in its life. Under those circumstances we highly recommend stripping off the existing finish.

PAINT REMOVAL

We like to see paint removed by chemical means or by the new soda blasting or plastic media blasting removal methods. We never recommend overall sand blasting because of the hydrogen embrittlement and the heat generated by silica sand. It can warp panels on new cars, literally warp them. Particularly on motorcycle parts we see the fenders get twisted from the heat. It doesn't mean that it can't be done with sand but you need to get a blasting company that's willing to turn their pressure down and then not stay on one area too long.

Plastic media doesn't warp anything (for more on plastic blasting see the S-10

Plastic blasting is a good way to remove paint - but not rust - with a low pressure stream of plastic particles.

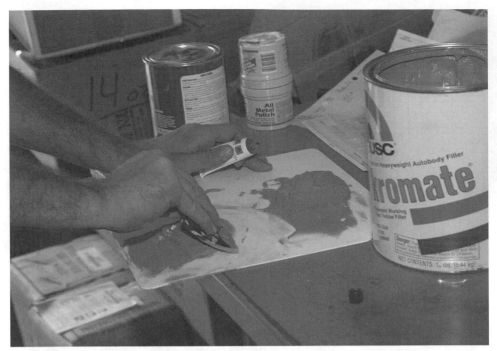

It's important to use a good brand of plastic filler and to mix it thoroughly so the hardener is evenly distributed.

Once you've applied the plastic filler you need to shape it with either a mud hog or straight-line sander.

project in chapter 6) but the plastic media doesn't remove rust, so if there's rust, you're either going to have get in there with a grinder or get in there with a motor-driven wire brush to get that rust. Obviously a bead blasting cabinet is excellent for that type of thing. For frame-off restorations the electro-chemical stripping does a good job.

BODYWORK AND USE OF FILLER

Once you're satisfied that you have the body panels where you want them in terms of the metal work, then you can begin doing the body filler work. One of the things we are conscious of throughout the entire process, from the time that it's stripped or blasted, is to keep our bare hands off the object. That means if it's a bike frame and fenders, you're always carrying them with a rag in your hand. You're never making bare skin contact which could affect adhesion of plastic filler and primers, this is true throughout the job, until you're to the point where you're color sanding or rubbing out the paint, and by then we're not going to be recoating again.

We have to be constantly conscious of the fact that our hands transfer oil.

Once we get into our body work the first thing is to prepare the areas that you can visually see for the plastic filler. You need to take care of that. Obviously, we

There are various ways to gauge the condition of the filler, but the best is a trained hand.

And once you've got the filler looking and feeling pretty good you might want to apply a guide coat of dark lacquer primer and start block sanding.

know there's going to be some spots that show up when we begin our block sanding, because that's what guide coats are about. But get your body work done first. I generally recommend using power equipment to prepare the metal so you get a good "tooth." Not that the bead blasting isn't going to prepare it somewhat, but there's nothing wrong with going over it with some 40 grit or 24 grit sanding pads to get a good tooth in the metal. You have to be care-

By block sanding across the guide coat (always in an X pattern) you take off the high spots - and the low spots show up as dark areas.

ful with the new thinner steels though not to spend a lot of time in one area. These new metals don't take the heat very well, so you have to keep the grinding with a coarse pad to a minimum.

Then mix the plastic filler well. Don't mix air into it, that means by squeegying it out on the mixing pad with alternating strokes: hard, low, medium, hard, light, medium, light, medium, low, hard. Working the air bubbles out and mixing the two-part material very thoroughly is very important. And remember which ever way you pull the plastic filler is the direction it will go. If I'm trying to fill a dent, and I keep pulling from the left to the right, I'm going to move that filler to the right. I have to turn around in the middle and make at least one or two pulls from the right to left in order to center the plastic filler and get it where I want it.

The smoother that you can put that filler on and the more evenly, the easier and quicker the sanding job will go. I like to file with a half round shredder. They're available in 14 inch, that's the size that I generally use. By going in and straight line pulling and X-ing from the right to the left, from the left to the right, drawing an invisible X

At House of Kolor we make two, two-part primers. This KP-2 is our kwik cure material. Our primers combine the tenacious bonding abilities of the best zinc chromate primer with the high solids and easy sanding of a good primer-surfacer.

through the center of that work, I can get the plastic filler very close to where I want it. When I'm close to where I want it, then I take my mud hog or DA sander (you could also use a powered straight line sander), and start sanding. I prefer a mud hog because it moves slower and gives you more control.

We then work with 36 or 40 grit and get it very, very close to where we want it to be with the machine. Then we come in with our long, skinny block using the same methods we did with the shredder. We use straight line back and forth and then X-ing from right to left, left to right, maintaining the block from the front to the rear of the vehicle. This way we can get the shape very, very close to where we want it to be.

Someone asked, "Can I use a finer paper to take the 40 grit scratches out of my plastic work?" I don't recommend going very heavy duty with 80, but you can use some 80 grit to knock down the high points. Do not spend a lot of time with the 80 grit, particularly while you're in the middle on steel, because when you run your hand over it with a rag in your hand, you'll be able to feel the difference where you leave the filler and go into the metal, and you don't want that. That means cutting it in with a little bit coarser grit, knocking the high points down with 80, but don't spend a lot of time with the 80.

Then blow it off very well and proceed throughout the job until we're ready to put primer on.

If you insist on using a metal etching material, which I don't really feel is necessary, make sure that you read and follow the label instructions. If it's not mixed correctly, it will actually do the

Our EP-2 has the same bonding abilities and sanding characteristics as the KP-2, but takes longer to cure. EP-2 is especially well suited to specialized substrates like fiberglass and aluminum.

reverse of what it's intended to do and cause the primer to flake off the steel. In many cases, particularly after a vehicle has been blasted like this, I don't get involved with using the metal etching materials. Though you might need Galva-prep on the rockers and certain galvanized panels on some of the new vehicles.

After the body is stripped, apply our two-part primer, our EP-2 or KP-2. These primers contain zinc chromate and have tremendous adhesion to a variety of materials including steel, aluminum, magnesium, galvanized, fiberglass and some plastics. (Be sure to read the notes on aluminum, magnesium and fiberglass farther along in this chapter.) The base (or primer) is the key to a good long-lasting job. This job is going to last a decade if it's well cared for. The foundation is the key.

What we generally recommend is three wet coats on the entire vehicle with extra coats of the

primer on the body work. Normally we start by putting our coats of EP-2 or KP-2 on the body work. These are wet coats and we allow each coat to flash solvent before we come in with the next coat (in the case of primers you will note they lose gloss as they flash).

Flashing of solvents on primers and base coats, top coats and clear coats is extremely important. Most painters get going so fast that they literally lock the solvents in with fast application of coat after coat. This causes a very much retarded dry and hardening times for these products. We see it happening all the time, particularly in the base coats and primer coats. It's extremely important to allow for the proper flash times.

This primer is an excellent first choice primer. Not only does it build well and sand like a lacquer primer, but it doesn't shrink if you allow the proper dry time. If you're one of the painters that likes

Because both our KP-2 and EP-2 contain zinc chromate they can both be used successfully on aluminum like these cast aluminum Harley-Davidson wheels. With either of

our primers you need to be sure to allow for flash times between coats so you don't trap solvents.

to prime in the morning and paint in the afternoon, you're not going to survive because your jobs are going to show it two weeks down the road. When they get in the first hot day your jobs are going to shrink up even if you have cut and buffed. You're going to wind up doing it again.

THE HOUSE OF KOLOR METHOD

So here's how we do it. We put two wet coats of our two-part primer on the body work with flash times between each coat. Then we put three coats on the whole vehicle.

By the way, when you're applying the primer is the time to start engineering the painting of that vehicle. Start looking at the tapering of the sheet metal. Start drawing invisible straight lines in the object. Don't converge your passes. Walk the length of the vehicle. Do things the way you're going to do them when you final paint the car. So you begin now training yourself for how you're going to apply the paint on this vehicle.

I don't believe that a primer gun should weigh twice what it did when it came from the factory. That means you must keep your equipment clean and working well. Measure everything that you do, that includes the mixing of the primer, to make sure that it's properly stirred. Stir the individual components carefully before mixing them together. If you have a shaker, that's ideal. If

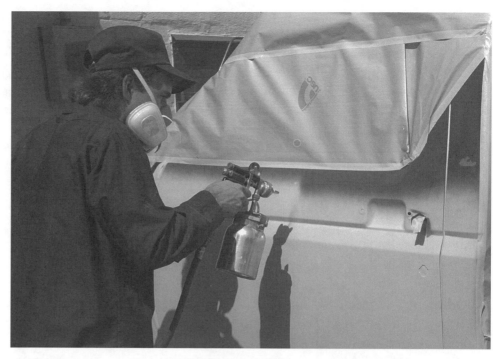

Don't be sloppy when you apply the primer, use the same precision that you would for final paint. Look at the primer as a practice session, a chance to engineer the paint job and learn all the quirks of painting this particular vehicle.

If you're going to paint it black and you intend to make it shine then the prep work had better be good. Because nothing shows off the ripples in the body work like a shiny black paint job.

49

you don't then spend the quality bench time getting that filler, there is filler in both the A and B side, mixed thoroughly. The EP-2 requires a 30 minute incubation time. That means when the A and B are mixed together you must wait 30 minutes before adding the reducer, stir them well of course but it needs this pre-reacted time.

The KP-2 is already pre-reacted and that's one of the reasons that it dries so much faster than the EP-2. There is no incubation time required on the KP-2 primer. You simply mix the two components, stir them well and strain them into the paint gun. After the primer coat flashes on the body work, then we put a complete coat on the car. We are starting to train ourselves. Take the tape measure and figure out the width at the back of the hood, the width at the front of the hood, and use straight line thinking to figure out the spray pattern. You have to follow straight lines,

you can't have the passes converge where the panel gets narrow. We recommend that 50 percent of the pattern overlap (there are a few exceptions to this rule). So if you've got a 6 inch pattern that means that gun must move over three inches with each coat that you make.

You have to be as organized as you can be. Where the sheet metal turns, put a coat on the curve of the metal. If it curves from a high point down to a low point follow that curve. That's called banding. We begin to do banding on these areas where they need it. For example, on an old car, you can't run right off the hood and down the front of the hood. You go off the roll of the front of the hood, and your next pass when you cross the front of the hood is to catch that curve of the sheet metal with one wet pass and then draw invisible straight lines with the area that's left and fill that in. We want to put the primer on with a

A perfect paint job like the one on this Dave Perewitz Harley-Davidson requires perfect preparation - to get maximum color from the final paint, to make sure there

are no imperfections that show up after the final paint is applied and to ensure the paint job lasts a long time.

nice even millage.

I know many painters tend to get very casual with the application of their primer coats. I don't get casual with anything. Because not only is it a waste of product, it changes the millage, and this is the time we start programming ourselves to paint this vehicle and do it right.

We walk the length of the side remembering to maintain the proper air cap angle to the vehicle, and that means perpendicular and vertical as well. That way we're not sweeping as we reach with the gun. We want to use wrist action to keep the gun dead parallel from right to left as well as from top to bottom. I particularly like to angle up at body grooves rather than down at the groove. It's amazing with a slight tip of the gun how fast you can put a run in an area by hitting it wrong as you go by. These things are often learned during the priming phase. It's certainly not a lesson you want

to learn when we begin putting on our high-quality final paint job.

And hold the gun close. So many painters get too far away. They're putting paint in the air. We want the paint on the vehicle. Obviously the new guns, the gravity feeds, that are designed specifically for primer work excellently. But some of the old siphon guns work just as well depending on the orifice size. For primer, we want a .070 inch minimum (70/1000). Some of the HVLPs obviously work best with a 1.7, a 1.9, a 2.3, whatever it might take for you to feel comfortable with the gun.

You need to watch the paint going on. You need to put on nice wet coats. Two on the body work and three on the overall sheet metal. That gives us 3 mils of primer on the car, 5 mils of primer on the body work areas. Then we come in with our guide coat. If we're using the EP-2 (at

Each step of the preparation is important. First you need good body work, then multiple coats of primer with plenty of block sanding, then a good wipe down in preparation for the sealer coat.

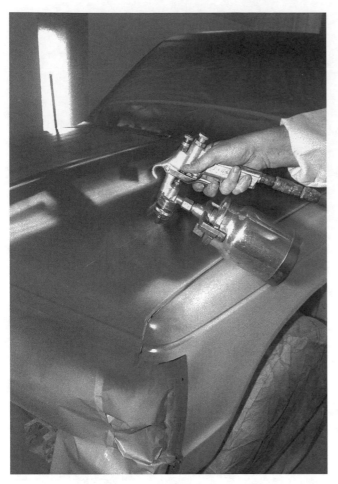

The sealer is normally applied in one coat and not sanded. It will aid adhesion, make the car one color and ensure that the topcoats don't soak down into the primer.

With EP-2 if you do happen to save some, simply bring it out of the refrigerator, stir it well, put it in a shaker or whatever, bring it to room temperature. If it goes through a strainer and looks alright it is totally usable at that later date. Some thinning can be done to the EP-2 using our EP-3 reducer. We don't recommend thinning the KP-2 at all due to the specialized type of catalyst that's in there, it is slightly thinner as produced.

We allow this KP-2, for example, to sit twelve to twenty four hours, actually fourteen to twenty four hours is ideal. There's no reason not to allow this dry time. We know it's going to eliminate shrinkage in future times. We don't want to see the job drying back on us, and the curing of the primer is a very critical item. One of the advantages of our primers is that they are extremely flexible and have tremendous elongation before crack-

seventy degrees) we might want to wait a couple of days, even three days, before we sand it.

Remember, any time that the epoxy is brought into temperatures below 60 degrees the dry times are almost eliminated. It will sit there dormant until it reaches these temperatures before it cures. So don't take a vehicle out of a warm area and put it in a cold storage area and assume it's going to dry in that area. It's not going to.

When you move the vehicle to a cool area the solvents and the dry times are going to be dormant, as proven by the fact the left over EP-2 can be put in the refrigerator and kept for weeks. This works with many two-part primers. It does not work with our KP-2, however, because the KP-2 is pre-reacted and even in the refrigerator will begin to thicken and lump up and is not usable the next day. Only mix what you can spray of the KP-2.

Polyester glaze is a two-part product and much better than the old one-part "spot putties." Use this in situations where you don't need (or don't want to use) plastic filler

ing. The EP-2, of course, is better than the KP-2, and it's the one that we recommend, particularly on fiberglass cars. We have seen cars painted 15 years ago with lacquer candy jobs, using this primer, and today they have no cracks, not even stress cracks. These materials tend to move with the body and don't tend to give up as fast as the old-style lacquer primers or many other companies two-part primers. (Note, KP-2, applied in *one medium coat*, can be top-coated in 60 to 90 minutes.)

Actually, if I've had a car media blasted, I'll sometimes take 80 grit and buzz the car quickly. Just to put a "scratch" in it. You've got to remember that two coats of the EP-2 or KP-2 will fill 24 grit scratches. This is a 70 percent solids, high-filling primer that sands easily. There are many two-part primers out there. Many of them sand like a brick. This stuff sands like the old-style lacquer primers. Only it's a high quality, two-part primer that's not going to shrink and not going move when you start putting on the paint.

When does a job fail? It begins to fail when you start putting on the wet coats and the primer starts to move because it wasn't a catalyzed primer, or maybe something will bleed through from underneath.

We do see some bleed-through bondo-leaching problems. It is important that no lacquer putties are

Use of good primer is especially important on motorcycles, because no matter now careful you are there will be gas spilled on the tank sooner or later. Note, with bikes it's important to mask off the area where the cap seals, so the gas cap gasket rests against bare metal.

I prefer to use a mud hog, to shape the plastic filler. It's fast and it gives you a feel for the shape of the mud even as you're working.

The Different Types of Primer

As we've stated repeatedly, the finest candy paint job in the world won't last long if the preparation and materials used under the finish paint aren't of the highest quality. Painters often think primer is just primer. Wrong. Primer comes in lacquer, two-part (often known as epoxy primer), urethane and polyester bases. There are pure primers, primer-surfaces and sealers.

PRIMER

A true primer is a paint material chosen for its good adhesion to the material it is sprayed over. Pure primer must provide good resistance to corrosion and moisture. A true primer generally is not meant to be sanded and contains a low percentage of solids.

PRIMER-SURFACER

Primer-surfacers are primer materials with a high solids content. While offering good adhesion like a straight primer, a primer-surfacer will help fill small scratches and imperfections, and sands easily. Primer-surfacers should be applied in two or three coats and then sanded when dry. If you fail to allow the material to dry properly before sanding, it will shrink *after* you've finished painting, allowing sand scratches to show through the finish paint job.

EPOXY PRIMER

An epoxy (or two-part) primer like our EP-2 or KP-2 is a high quality, durable, primer material. These paints are known for their superior bonding abilities, great corrosion resistance and flexibility. The catalyst in these paints is not an isocyanate.

Our EP-2 and KP-2 can be sanded like a primer-surfacer yet these materials bonds strongly with the base substrate and may be used as the first material sprayed over bare steel, aluminum, magnesium, fiberglass and some plastics.

PRIMER-SEALER

A primer-sealer, sometimes known as a sealer, is meant to do three things: Act as a bond coat between primer and topcoats, Act as holdout agent to prevent topcoats from soaking into the primer and reducing gloss, and most important, sealers make the object to be painted all one color for faster coverage with the final topcoats, reducing the material and labor needed for the paint job.

ADHESION PROMOTER

Adhesion promoters like our AP-01 are similar in intent to primer-sealers and are sometimes used to ensure that one coat of paint will stick to another coat or material underneath.

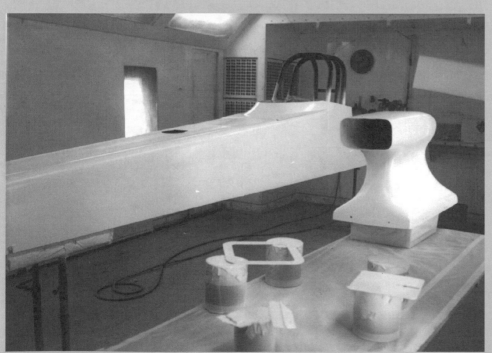

This is Mike's dragster in basecoat, sprayed over KP-2 primer. As paint jobs like this one get more complex they also get thicker, meaning more and more layers of paint all depending on the primer as the foundation for the whole job.

used. You must use a catalyzed putty if a putty is required for some deep scratches or low spots. Most of those are considered stain free. Like plastic filler it's important that they be mixed properly.

Then we use our guide coat. One of the rare times we will use lacquer is for a guide coat. We will use a lacquer primer; a dark contrasting primer. We will dust a coat on over the primer that we've applied and this gives us our guide. In other words, by using a block and very carefully pressing the block down and moving it slowly back and forth and X-ing it, it will show us our low points. It will show us our scratches in our plastic filler, and we can progress and eliminate these scratches and sand no further than necessary to eliminate all of the guide coat.

We'd like to see at least 2 mils of primer remaining on this vehicle before we begin our painting. We know that this primer is going to prevent our plastic filler from bleeding through because we have specialized additives in there that will prevent this. You don't see that with other companies' two-part primers. We have the additives - we know they work.

We're not going in there and dealing with your average three mil finished paint job here. We are putting on a 10-12 plus mil paint job. And with art work we constantly see the jobs going to 15 mils and living for years and years and years because we've designed these products specifically for custom painting

and they are designed to withstand this millage and live. If everything is done according to our instructions you're just not going to see problems with these products.

All right, now we will go ahead and sand everything. One of the problems we hear often is that a painter will sand the primer with too fine a sandpaper because he's doing a *custom* paint job. He thinks he has to do things different. You must remember with a catalyzed primer that there is no such thing as a chemical bite because these primers are chemically resistant. Which means that you must have a mechanical bond between the final paint and the primer. That's the two types of adhesion - chemical or mechanical. What we look for here, if you're dry-sanding with a DA sander, a 240 or a 280 grit works great. If you're wet sanding, we like to see a 400 grit and we never go finer than 400 grit wet for the final sanding.

This is what we do. We go in and prepare

More complexity means more labor (and money). The primer had better be good because if it fails you've spent all that time and money for nothing.

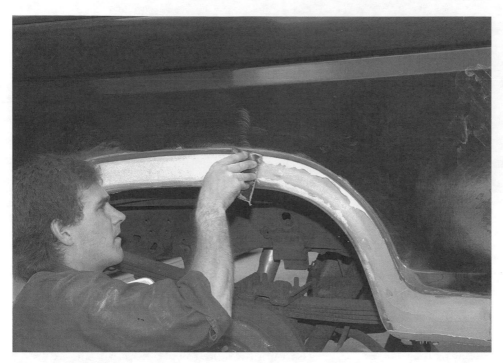

It makes sense to apply and shape the plastic filler carefully and save the labor of having to sand off all that material you didn't really need.

everything. Do it right. You can get the long paper for your block if you want to wet sand. Many painters will dry sand but I do think you get a better sand with wet sanding. Then we will wipe it all down. Use a final wash solvent. Remember, tar, wax, and grease remover is used for removing tar, wax, and grease from a factory finish. It is rarely used during the paint job. Unless it specifies on the label that it may be used for final wash. But even those that do don't tell you that sometimes they're using a derivative of kerosene, which is an oil base, and we really prefer not to see final washes used unless they're designed and intended to be used as a final wash.

We final wash the job and now we are ready to apply our seal coats. The sealer is available in varied colors which is one of the primary things we want to do - pick a sealer that's going to work well underneath our particular base color. Don't put a red oxide down if you're going to spray a silver metallic base, because they don't go together. Whereas a light gray sealer will allow you to get your three-coat coverage very quickly and evenly, and then we can proceed.

The other thing a sealer does is improve the adhesion between the base, or sanded primer, and our topcoats. That only works providing that the label instructions have been followed explicitly. If the sealer gets

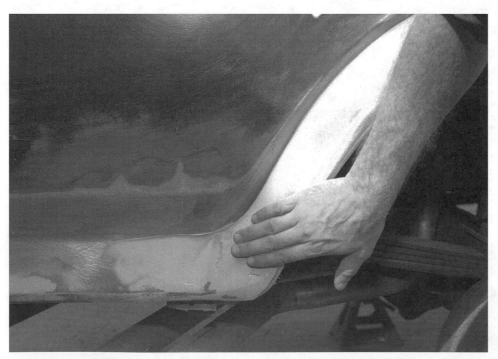

Your hand is a very sensitive tool for checking the shape of a panel. Check your work often, you might want to use a rag between your hand and the panel as it helps to accentuate any high and low spots.

too dry it will not be receptive to the paint. I had a customer call one day, and he said, "I put my sealer on last weekend, and I'm going to paint this weekend." When you do that, you must completely wet sand all of the sealer and re-seal it because you have lost the bonding feature by allowing it to dry too long. That means the paint will not bite into it properly. There is a window of time after application of a sealer when you can apply the final paint. Be sure to follow the recommendation on the label.

The other thing a sealer does is prevents the top coats from soaking into the primer (our Ko-seal contains barytes which helps make it chemically resistant). But that isn't really going to help us much in this case because we have a chemical resistant primer so we're not going to get any penetration. But it would help in the case where you're applying final paint over a lacquer primer.

Now we're ready to put our top coats on. Once you apply the sealer be ready to go. Because once we put our sealer on we're committed to our base coat and to our top coats. If it's a basecoat, clearcoat system; that goes very quickly. If it's a basecoat, kandycoat, clearcoat system, we have to be committed to that. We have to know we have enough time in the work day to complete a job or don't start it. Don't get interrupted

It's important to be neat and always wipe off the panels before painting, even during the primer stages.

Because there was only one layer of paint on the truck and it was in good condition, we chose to sand the existing paint instead of stripping the whole truck.

during the paint job. If something should happen - if you get interrupted during the paint job, a lot of weird things can happen if you come back and try to re-coat after a certain amount of time. Pay attention to that as you go through this book on how we use this material. How we apply each and every product, and what you have to look out for and what you should do in order to make it work right.

PREPARATION OF SPECIALIZED SUBSTRATES
PREPARE AND PAINT FIBERGLASS

I'm always asked about fiberglass, people say, "I've got a new fiberglass '32 Ford or '36 Ford

> **…most of the companies that manufacture fiberglass bodies use a water-borne mold-release agent. So the very first thing you want to do with that new body is scrub it with hot soapy water and a scrub brush.**

roadster, what do I do with my fiberglass car before I apply the primer?"

The very first thing you need to know is that most of the companies that manufacture fiberglass bodies use a water-borne mold-release agent. So the very first thing you want to do with that new body is scrub it with hot soapy water and a scrub brush. It doesn't make any difference if you put a scratch in the gel-coat, because we're going to do a lot more than that by the time we're done. We scrub it down with hot water and some good detergent and a good scrub brush. You can use every solvent known to man and it will not take off the release agents, but soap and water will. If you sand it

If you're in doubt about the thickness or condition of the existing paint (especially if it's a series of small parts)

there's only one thing to do - strip it down to the bare metal and start over.

before you do this there's a good chance that you will grind this wax-like material into the surface of the gel-coat and have a difficult time getting it out. A very important first move.

Once you have washed the body then I come in with a solvent wash, either a final wash solvent or a tar, wax, and grease remover. Then I will take my DA sander with 80 grit, and I will scratch the gel-coat thoroughly. I want to knock off all of the shine prior to application of the primer, preferably EP-2 on the fiberglass. I know it takes a longer cure time, but believe me when I tell you that the two, three, four days that you wait for this primer to cure will add years and years to the life of your paint job. It's been proven. We've been making this primer since the mid 1960's and it's a proven winner.

PREPARE AND PAINT ALUMINUM

With aluminum all you want to do is scratch the back of the aluminum lightly. They do make an aluma-prep that you can use for etching to get improved adhesion. Then apply your zinc chromate epoxy, preferably the EP-2 on aluminum (KP-2 works too), and you're ready to sand after the given dry times. It also works well on magnesium but there are some specialized preparation treatments for magnesium so be sure to call and check before you start painting magnesium.

IN THE END

You might think that primer is just a step you have to get out of the way as fast as possible so you can move on to the "real" painting. But if your primer isn't a quality product and it isn't applied with care, the final paint either won't look good or won't have any longevity. So treat the primer application with the same attention to detail that you would the kandy colors or the final clearcoat.

In the " good old days" we had to do our custom paint jobs over lacquer primer, which didn't have the durability and chemical resistance of our current two-part primers.

When it comes to custom painting it keeps getting easier because the products keep getting better.

Chapter Four

Final Paint Application

Dirt, the real enemy of a quality paint job

Before starting on the final paint, you have to remember that dirt is a real problem. Eliminate the dirt and you've eliminated the problem. We go through a number of steps before we ever pull the trigger on the gun, all to make sure that vehicle is as clean and dust free as we can make it.

Ideally a good pressure washing the night

We make our colors in both a lacquer and a urethane base, though we sell less and less lacquer each year.

before you're going to begin the final painting is an excellent way to get in all the crevices and areas that might hold dirt. There's a system called the Folex System that takes the rubbers around the windows and holds them away from the vehicle before you mask. I highly recommend using that. It's a little expensive, but then there's no paint on the rubbers which is an excellent way to go.

The next step is a final wash and make sure you're not using a tar, wax, and grease remover because some of those contain oily compounds or refined kerosene which will leave a residue behind. You want to make sure that your final wash is marked that way and that it's designed as a final wash for the primer. Then, of course, blow the object off with air and tack it. Either use the new style of throw away wipes, made with paper that actually feel like a cloth and they're lint free, or get some good shop rags from a rental place. That's the way we usually do it, we wipe the vehicle off with a cloth that we wet with final wash. Then we blow it off good with high pressure air and wipe it down with a tack rag.

I usually blow the vehicle off twice, first with

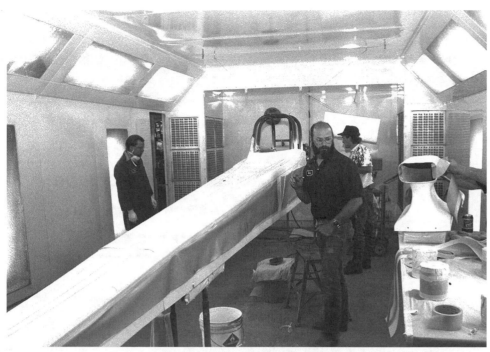

A complex paint job like the one we put on the dragster requires careful planning. You have to decide what you want for the final product and then plan backwards so each step leaves you prepared for the next one.

Before you put down the sealer the car should be wiped down with a final wash product - one that really is a final wash and will leave no oily residues behind.

direct air out of the compressor - with the booth fan running - making sure you're going through a good final filter so you're not transferring any oil from the compressor through your compressor lines which can cause fish eyes and other contaminants. Always make sure to keep anything that contains silicone out of the shop so you don't have any chance of contamination.

After we've done the high speed, high pressure air blow down and a wipe with the tack cloth then we allow the booth to sit and calm down with the booth fan running. Then we switch the air to regulated normal pressure that we're going to spray the car with and we go back in again

and blow the car off with low pressure air and tack the car again. Then we let it set for a short period of time, usually as long as it takes to mix the paint. When we go back into the booth to paint we do a final tack.

A painter's suit is highly recommended. General Motors ran some tests to determine where most of the dirt in their paint jobs came from and most of it comes from the painter's clothing. Either a disposable or a quality painter's suit is a good thing.

THE PAINT BENCH

I also think the paint bench is extremely important. By that I mean measuring all the

> **You need accurate measurements according to the label instructions (which you *must* read) on the can.**

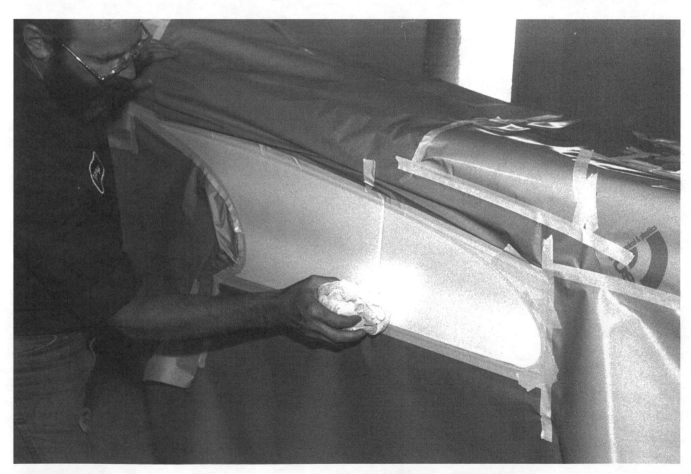

A tack rag should be the last thing you do before pulling the trigger, especially in taped out areas where it's hard to use a liquid cleaner. Always let a new tack rag "air" first before using it on the vehicle.

products that you're working with. You need accurate measurements according to the label instructions (which you *must* read) on the can. If catalyst is required use it and be sure it's the right one.

SEALER

Then we begin our seal coats. Usually it's a good idea to use the fine strainers when you're straining sealer. Many times sealers have barytes or other fillers in them which can sometimes get lumpy when they sit around. Very carefully strain everything, even the primer should be strained. So many people think it's not important because they're going to sand the primer but it's the beginning of a quality paint job.

Now we've got our sealer applied following the label instructions on the sealer. We let it sit generally 30 to 40 minutes, not over an hour, and then we come in with our basecoat, or if it's going to be a solid color, we begin whichever is required at that stage based on the product and label instructions.

GUN ADJUSTMENTS AND HANDLING

Before you start the final application, it's always a good idea to go through gun adjustments.

Every gun is different. There are a number of nozzle, needle, air cap combinations, particularly on the new HVLPs. Some work better for basecoats; others are excellent for clearcoats. You have to fully understand the gun you've chosen.

Our pearls come in a variety of forms. These PBC Pearl Base Coats are part of our Shimrin line meaning they go on easy with medium coats and dry fast. You can either topcoat these with clear or get more creative and use them as a base under a kandy color with a final clearcoat.

We very rarely recommend pulling the trigger all the way. We always like the fan left wide. By restricting the material control (or trigger pull) we can set the pattern to the width that we want based on a particular gun distance. You must know the distance between the gun and the object you're painting. We really don't like to see the gun get much further than seven inches away from the object being painted. In many cases, particularly on bases, we'll work even closer than that.

Then you have to ascertain what your pattern overlap is. Once you've determined your fan width, then you can determine what your overlap or increment of overlap is. That is, how far you're going to move the gun after each pass. That has to be as accurate as possible. We're not splitting hairs here, we're not talking about rocket science. But so many painters go back and forth in the same place.

And the gun must always be kept as parallel as possible to the work. Obviously, if you tip it up one way or the other the pattern is going to become heavier on one side. It's important to draw invisible straight lines through the object that's being painted so you don't get tricked up into following body lines or making special emphasis on creases in the body work or whatever happens to be there because this can cause runs.

There's also a term called banding, which simply means you must always put a pass with the

A painter's suit not only keeps you healthy but also keeps the lint on your clothes out of the paint for a better job and minimal color sanding.

gun on the curve where the sheet metal bends. That's the only time you disregard the straight line theory. Whenever the sheet metal bends, like on the side of a fender, comes off the hood, goes to the fender, and turns and goes down the side of the vehicle, that's a banding situation. But after you've done your banding, then you have to think straight lines again from that banding point so you're not crossing over.

I always tell painters, "If you want to know the reason for a run in something that you've painted, go look in the mirror, because it's you. It's something that you've done, the way that you've handled the paint application." We always kid painters when they call and tell us that they got a run in the job, we say, "Oh, you must have got one of our cans with a run in it." Obviously, that's not the case. There is no such thing as a can with a run in it. Maybe your pattern is not accurate. Maybe the gun's been dropped after you used it last, and it's not putting out an even pattern. We always want to check our gun pattern on a piece of cardboard or some paper taped on the booth wall so you know exactly what the gun is doing.

I like to see painters use a tape measure to determine gun distance and the width of the pattern. That way once the gun is set up you know what your increment of overlap is going to be. If you're pulling the trigger too hard (or have the material knob set too rich) with certain bases, particularly pearl bases, you can blotch the first coat and it'll take you two or three extra coats to get those blotches out and

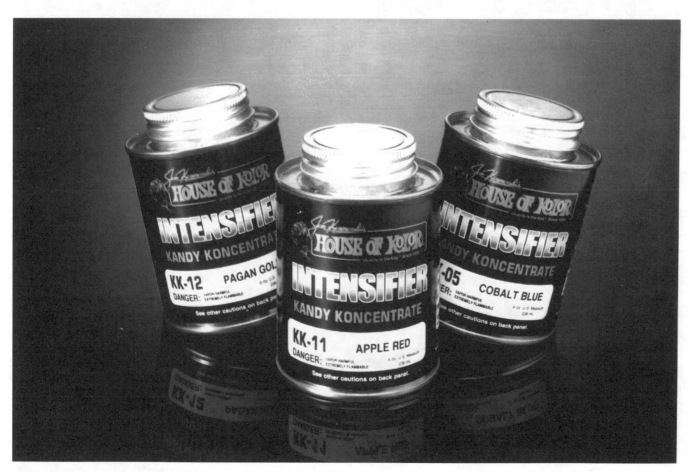

The KK products are Kandy Koncentrates, used to mix your own kandy with SG-100 or to strengthen our existing kandys for faster coverage.

Inside The Paint Can

Paint, any paint, is made up of three basic components: pigment, resin and solvent, as well as a few additives.

Pigment is the material that gives the paint it's color. Though older paints often used lead-based pigments all the modern paints from House of Kolor have been converted to non-lead pigments. Resin (also known as Binder) helps to hold the pigments together and keep them sticking to the metal. Solvent is the carrier used to make the paint thin enough to spray. In the case of lacquers a true thinner is used while in the case of an enamel the solvent is called a reducer.

Additives are materials added to the paint to give it a certain property or help it overcome a problem much the way that additives are incorporated into modern oils to improve their performance.

Going back to the three basic components of paint, the solvent (a volatile material) evaporates (or oxidizes) after the paint is sprayed leaving behind the pigment and binder, known as the solids. Solvents that evaporate into the atmosphere are known in the industry as VOCs and have come under government regulation in many areas.

THE MAJOR KINDS OF PAINT

Automotive paints can be classified as either a lacquer, an enamel or a urethane. At house of Kolor, we manufacture both urethane and lacquer based products. Our Shimrin basecoats can be topcoated with either lacquer or urethane kandies and clears. These Shimrins are actually a unique combination of acrylic urethane and copolymers that behave like lacquer but far surpass lacquer in lasting performance.

LACQUER

Lacquer paints have been available for years and years. During the 1950s, I painted hundreds of custom cars and bikes with lacquer, nitrocellulose lacquer to be exact. Today we offer acrylic lacquer for painters who need a lacquer based product.

Custom painters have always liked lacquer because of it's fast drying times, low toxicity, great color and the ease

JON KOSMOSKI'S
HOUSE OF KOLOR inc.
"Quality is the Key Since 1956."®

TECH SHEETS

Our House of Kolor Tech Sheets are available just by calling our tech line. There is no charge and they contain a tremendous amount of information on each of our products.

TECH - 05 — SHIMRIN® DESIGNER PEARLS (PBC) & SHIMRIN® UNIVERSAL PEARLESCENT (PC)

GENERAL INFORMATION — *READ ALL INSTRUCTIONS BEFORE YOU BEGIN.*
SHIMRIN Designer Pearls (PBC) are universal base coats that may simply be cleared for a final finish, or used as a base coat for Kandys. Due to their unique chemistry make-up, they may be topcoated with either acrylic lacquer or urethane enamel. Once a system is chosen (acrylic lacquer or urethane enamel) use only products within that system. *Intermixing of these two systems, after the base coat, is not recommended.* For example: If SHIMRIN Pearl is topcoated with an acrylic lacquer Kandy, it must also be cleared with an acrylic lacquer clear.
NOTE: Earlier SHIMRIN Bases were packaged with a Kosmic Kolor Urethane Enamel label, but we are gradually changing to the new SHIMRIN label.

IMPORTANT NOTE — Bleeding from underneath is the most common problem when painting with pearls. Follow instructions carefully and protect yourself against failure. Good preparation is important for a quality, long-lasting paint job.

1. PREPARATION — Prepare vehicle using normal custom painting methods for acrylic lacquer or urethane. Use only medium or hi-solid catalyzed primers over bodywork. Pearl bases are very susceptible to staining or bleeding from plastic fillers, putties, fiberglass resins and some primers. To prevent staining, strip bare (or to OEM primer) and prime with our EP-2 Epoxy Primer or our KP-2 Kwikure Epoxy Primer. *See tech sheet 12 for more information on EP-2 and KP-2.* For additional information consult **Kustom Painting Secrets** (book or video).

2. SEALER — *UNIFORM COVERAGE OF SEALER OR PRIMER IS REQUIRED BEFORE APPLICATION OF BASE COAT.* Use a sealer recommended for acrylic lacquer or urethane enamel, such as our Ko-seal (available in three colors). Use a sealer closest to the base color for faster coverage of base coats. Follow label instructions. Allow flash time on sealer. *See tech sheet 13 for more information on Ko-seal.*
NOTE: Sealer is not a cure-all for poor preparation and does not prevent discoloration or bleeding. The main purpose of the sealer is to increase adhesion of topcoats, to make the object one color (nearest to the base for faster coverage), and to improve color holdout.

3. GROUND COAT — *VEHICLE MUST BE ONE EVEN COLOR BEFORE APPLICATION OF PEARL BASE COAT.* Use BC-26 White as a ground coat for white or light colored pearls (as shown on our Kustom Koatings color card). *The color of the ground coat will vary the final pearl color. This is an excellent place for creativity.* You may also use any of our Kosmic Kolor SHIMRIN Bases, Graphic Kolors or Neons, for the ground coat. Follow label instructions. Allow flash time on each coat of ground coat.
NOTE: Primers and sealers may also be used as a ground coat.

4. MIXING SHIMRIN DESIGNER PEARL (PBC) — *Stir SHIMRIN Pearl well. Reduce 50% (2 parts paint to 1 part reducer). Mix well. REDUCE ONLY WITH OUR KOSMIC REDUCERS.* Use the reducer best suited to your shop temperature. SHIMRIN Designer Pearls are formulated to self-orient the pearl platelets and freeze them into position so no mottling occurs when topcoated. *See tech sheet 12 for more information on reducers.*
NOTE: Kosmic Reducers are not cross-referenced by any other paint company.
When blending, you may slightly over-reduce SHIMRIN Designer Pearls or mix them with SG-100 Intercoat Clear for undetectable blends.
NOTE: Even though SHIMRIN Designer Pearls are the easiest to apply, equipment, spray technique and air pressure can affect the pearl distribution. A full trigger pull is normally not recommended.
NOTE: Splitting or cracking is possible when using other companies' reducers or by using a reducer that is too slow for your shop conditions. Splitting or cracking may also occur when painting too fast without allowing proper dry time or by pumping on the base too wet and heavy.

This technical listing for our Shimrin Pearls is typical and includes general information on use of the product, mixing instructions and application considerations.

with which spot repairs can be made. Custom painters often put lacquer on in multiple coats, wet sanding between coats. The end result is that classic deep shine.

The trouble with modern acrylic lacquer is it's lack of durability (it chips and stains easily) and the large amount of maintenance a lacquer paint job requires. The other problem with lacquer paints is the VOC issue. The evaporating thinner and the multiple coats (more thinner) means that spraying lacquer puts a relatively large amount of VOCs in the atmosphere.

URETHANE

Most of the custom painting being done today is being done with urethane. Technically, urethane like our Kosmic Kolor is an enamel, yet it sprays much like a lacquer. Urethane is a two-part paint material catalyzed with an iso-cyanate. Even though it's classed as an enamel, urethane dries very fast and offers easy spot repairs. The fast drying means quick application of second coats, easy candy paint jobs and fast tape outs for flame jobs and graphics. Unlike lacquer, urethane is super durable, resisting rock chips and chemical stains better than almost anything. We offer urethanes that you can use as a one shot application, as a basecoat-clearcoat or as a tri-coat system.

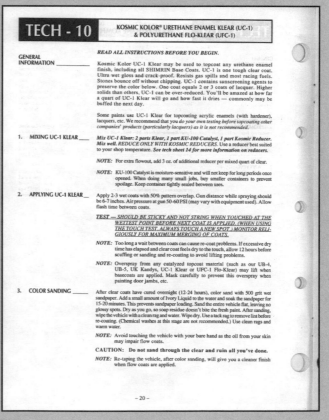

TECH - 10 — KOSMIC KOLOR® URETHANE ENAMEL KLEAR (UC-1) & POLYURETHANE FLO-KLEAR (UFC-1)

GENERAL INFORMATION — *READ ALL INSTRUCTIONS BEFORE YOU BEGIN.*
Kosmic Kolor UC-1 Klear may be used to topcoat any urethane enamel finish, including all SHIMRIN Base Coats. UC-1 is one tough clear coat. Ultra wet gloss and crack-proof. Resists gas spills and most racing fuels. Stones bounce off without chipping. UC-1 contains sunscreening agents to preserve the color below. One coat equals 2 or 3 coats of lacquer. Higher solids than others, UC-1 can be over-reduced. You'll be amazed at how far a quart of UC-1 Klear will go and how fast it dries — commonly may be buffed the next day.

Some paints use UC-1 Klear for topcoating acrylic enamels (with hardener), lacquers, etc. We recommend that you do your own testing before topcoating other companies' products (particularly acrylic lacquers) as it is not recommended.

1. MIXING UC-1 KLEAR — *Mix UC-1 Klear: 2 parts Klear, 1 part KU-100 Catalyst, 1 part Kosmic Reducer. Mix well. REDUCE ONLY WITH KOSMIC REDUCERS.* Use a reducer best suited to your shop temperature. *See tech sheet 14 for more information on reducers.*
NOTE: For extra flowout, add 3 oz. of additional reducer per mixed quart of clear.
NOTE: KU-100 Catalyst is moisture-sensitive and will not keep for long periods once opened. When doing many small jobs, buy smaller containers to prevent spoilage. Keep container tightly sealed between uses.

2. APPLYING UC-1 KLEAR — Apply 2-3 wet coats with 50% pattern overlap. Gun distance while spraying should be 6-7 inches. Air pressure at gun 50-60 PSI (may vary with equipment used). Allow flash time between coats.
TEST — SHOULD BE STICKY AND NOT STRING WHEN TOUCHED AT THE WETTEST POINT BEFORE NEXT COAT IS APPLIED. (WHEN USING THE TOUCH TEST, ALWAYS TOUCH A NEW SPOT.) MONITOR RELIGIOUSLY FOR MAXIMUM MERGING OF COATS.
NOTE: Too long a wait between coats can cause re-coat problems. If excessive dry time has elapsed and clear coat feels dry to the touch, allow 12 hours before scuffing or sanding and re-coating to avoid lifting problems.
NOTE: Overspray from any catalyzed topcoat material (such as our UB-4, UB-5, UK Kandys, UC-1 Klear or UFC-1 Flo-Klear) may lift when basecoats are applied. Mask carefully to prevent this overspray when painting door jambs, etc.

3. COLOR SANDING — After clear coats have cured overnight (12-24 hours), color sand with 500 grit wet sandpaper. Add a small amount of Ivory Liquid to the water and soak the sandpaper for 15-20 minutes. This prevents sandpaper loading. Sand the entire vehicle flat, leaving no glossy spots. Dry as you go, so soap residue doesn't take the fresh paint. After sanding, wipe the vehicle with a clean rag and water. Wipe dry. Use a tack rag to remove lint before re-coating. (Chemical washes at this stage are not recommended.) Use clean rags and warm water.
NOTE: Avoid touching the vehicle with your bare hand as the oil from your skin may impair flow coats.
CAUTION: Do not sand through the clear and ruin all you've done.
NOTE: Re-taping the vehicle, after color sanding, will give you a cleaner finish when flow coats are applied.

In addition to general information this tech sheet helps explain the differences between UC-1 (and UFC-1) and the other clears from our line.

you may lose some of the intensity of the pearl.

SHOP TEMPERATURE.

Make sure that you have a thermometer in your booth, check the temperature with the fan running, so you know what the temperature in your spray booth is. That way when you mix the paint you're using the right speed reducer or thinner so you get the proper dry time between coats. You don't want to be using products that dry very, very slowly and take way too long to dry because that can cause problems with the look of the job. You want everything to be on schedule as far as the dry time goes, you don't want to be going in there and pumping a wet coat on a wet coat.

In other words, if there isn't enough time for the solvents to flash out of the system, you can trap solvents and that's when you start to see die-back weeks after the job is done. Those solvents you trapped will still try to work their way out of the film and they will dull the paint job when they do. Measuring, adjusting the gun, timing between coats, engineering the object, walking the side of the car, these are all very important parts of your painting technique.

BASECOATS

Obviously the easiest way to go is with a basecoat, clearcoat. Simply put your basecoat down, get a nice even application and then let that flash for 15 or 20 minutes and come in with

You need to understand the gun you chose to use. This Sata gun uses this knob on the side to adjust the fan width. In addition to the two standard adjustments this gun has an air flow adjustment valve.

your clearcoats. Very simple to touch these up. We recommend a 75 percent overlap on the application of basecoats, because they're never applied wet. You always apply a base coat in what we call a medium coat. If you put a medium coat on with the gun too far away, you're going to stucco the job. You should be painting in the four to five to maximum six inch distance away from that vehicle, so that you're putting it on evenly but not wetting it - that way the proper orientation takes place, which the base coats are meant to do.

Now, of course, we have developed candy-basecoats that take on the candy look and they're much easier to apply than a straight candy. But then again, you still have to be careful with gun adjustments, gun distance and your basic application technique. There isn't anything made that somebody can't foul up by not paying attention or understanding the procedures required to do the work.

KANDY AND PEARLS

You have to be careful with gun distance and the adjustments when you apply our kandy kolors. If you're too far away blotchiness will take place. Or if you're pulling

the trigger too hard you'll get blotches and those blotches will follow you throughout the whole job. It does require some expertise in gun adjustments and understanding how to hold the gun.

A kandy is really a tinted clear. A very

The UFC-1 clear is one of our nicest clears (catalyzed with our KU-500 catalyst) with a long flowout and ultra-high gloss. This is a very flexible paint with tremendous stone and bruise resistance. With our clears you have to be sure to use the correct catalyst: The UC-1 uses KU-100 catalyst, the UFC-40 uses KU-400 catalyst and the UFC-80 is catalyzed with KU-800. All are reduced with our Kosmic reducers.

Our intensifiers (both the Neon Koncentrate and Kandy Koncentrate) are rich in pigments and allow the painter to mix colors and concentrates not commonly available. These can also be used to mix a stronger color for faster coverage.

strong pigment that holds up in small amounts and gives you that transparency through to the underbase. That's what translates to that extra depth that you see when you look into a candy paint job. It's a layering of color. Kandy layers and the clearcoats must be applied in a timely fashion, being careful to follow recommendations for flash times.

A pearl is like a very very small metallic, but the pearl paints have a tendency to glow in the light - you get that glow as light reflected back from the pearl platelets. We have pearls available in a number of different forms: powders, paste, pre-mixed, semi-transparent and interference pearls.

Adjusting the equipment is the key to getting the pearl on evenly too. And if you're doing pearl or kandy remember that the basecoat must be applied evenly first. We have information available on gun set up, we have over 65 paint guns in our shop. We spray with everybody's equipment so if you're not sure which air cap and needle to use, call our tech line for help (see the Sources at the back of the book). We are fairly knowledgeable with most everyone's equipment that's being used today.

KLEARS AND CLEARCOATS

Here at House of Kolor we now make four different clears. Depending on your VOC requirements, certain parts of the country now are getting very sensitive to volatile organic

A good paint job requires a clean air stream. The feed line should be at least 3/4 inch I.D. and the junctions should go up and then turn down to minimize passage of dirt into the paint gun. Filters and water traps should be located at the point where you attach the gun, not at the compressor.

compounds in the paints. But particularly if you're doing motorcycle work or you're doing work where you want a fast setting clear, maybe not the highest gloss, and maybe not the highest solids, but one that gets very hard overnight. We think this is important if you're doing artwork and you want to get a clear that will give you a good build up but be extremely hard the next day so that when you go to recoat you're not going to have shrinkage.

This particular clear, the UC-1, uses the same catalyst that goes into our candies, the KU-100, and it dries extremely hard the next day. You will look at left over paint on the bench that maybe you put into a container and you'll see that it's very hard the next day. Most other clears you use with catalyst in them will still pour out of their container the next day. The UC-1 is an excellent fuel-proof clear. It resists nitromethane fuels. It's got a solid content ready to spray of about 30 to 31 percent. As I said, it's not our highest percentage of solids clear, but it does get hard quickly. It's an excellent all around clear. It doesn't have the gloss, however, of our UFC-1 which is about a 39 or 40 percent solids clear. That's ready to spray again, once the catalyst and the reducer are mixed in, and these are all done with the 2:1:1 ratio. Two parts of clear, one part of catalyst, one part of reducer.

The reducer is the same in all of our products. The catalyst varies with different products. The UFC-1 uses the KU-

We've said it before: You have to keep the gun 90 degrees to the object, don't let the gun get too far away and be careful to keep the hose from touching the body. Engineer your painting so the center of the roof that you painted on the left side doesn't sit too long before you come along and paint the center of the roof from the right side.

After you've made one pass go back and make another, being careful to follow recommendations for overlap (commonly 50 percent for basecoats). When you start on the right side of the roof start in the center and work to the outside.

Paint Gun Adjustments

The paint gun is the painter's primary tool. In the case of a paint gun you must understand the tool and equip it with the right air cap, fluid nozzle and needle. You must also understand how to adjust the pattern on that gun.

The first thing we do is to set the fan control wide open. In most cases this is the top control knob and usually it means backing the knob out all the way. Sometimes called "air to the horns" this knob controls the amount of air to the outer orifices in the air cap and thus the shape of the fan.

Sometimes a "dot" pattern is useful for spraying a small area. To get the dot pattern (as illustrated) close the top adjustment (air to the horns) . It's important to remember that with the fan in this position you need to further limit the material, (or further restrict the trigger pull). A starting point for material control knob in a situation like this might be one turn out, then check the pattern and adjust accordingly. (You will probably want to reduce the air pressure as well.)

How you set the material knob will depend to a certain amount on your gun. With a conventional siphon gun we like to check the pattern with the material control

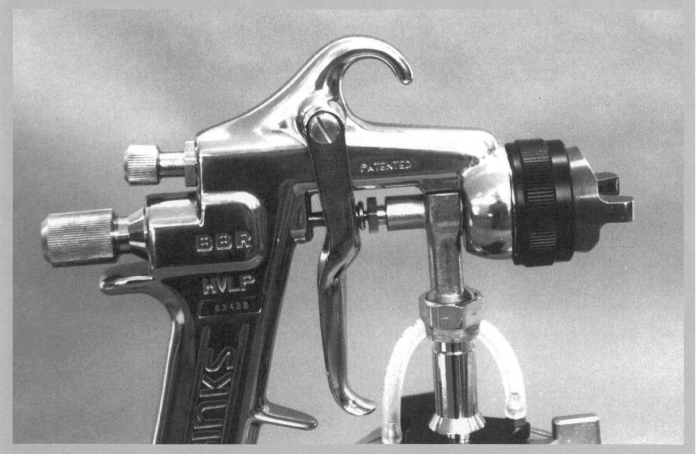

Spray guns with the adjustments in the "standard" location like this Binks use the upper knob to control air to the horns (which shape the fan). The lower knob controls the material or trigger pull.

knob (the lower one on most siphon guns) about two turns out.

FLUID TIP SIZE

For siphon-style guns a fluid tip I.D. between .062 and .070 inch is good for all around use. These sizes would work well for lacquer and low-solids base coats. Primer tips might be as big as .080 inch or larger. HVLP guns are different and painters should check with the manufacturer for a recommendation. Note, most HVLP guns use metric fluid tip sizes which convert as follows: 1.4 mm = .055 inch, 1.6 mm = .063 inch and 1.8 mm = .071.

With the upper knob wide open you got a nice wide fan as shown. We like to spray with the upper control open all the way and use the material knob (the lower adjustment on these guns) to give the pattern size required for the object being painted.

If you shut off the fan control (no air to the horns) then the pattern becomes a round dot. This is useful for painting certain hard to reach places. Remember that you will have to further restrict the material knob when you adjust the gun to a dot pattern - and you may also want to decrease the air pressure to the gun at the same time.

500 catalyst and you cannot intermix the catalysts. The dry times will not be accurate. There are radical differences in the way the catalysts are made. I get a kick out of painters who buy universal or after market generic catalysts and try to use them in our products. They find out very quickly that this is not the way to go. The savings is not worth the problems that you can encounter trying to use outside products.

That goes with our reducer as well. Our ingredients are the best in the industry. We don't take any short cuts. We don't use filler solvents. Ours is the best that money can buy. That's what equates to long lasting paint jobs. It's not uncommon for us to hear of paint jobs 15 years old, done with our products and still looking good.

Now we've come out with another clear for the VOC sensitive areas, and that's our UFC-40 which is 52 percent solids ready to spray. It uses the KU-400 catalyst. It's a beautiful clear.

All of these clears buff very easily. The UC-1 is the clear that you want to buff the next day. Don't let that clear set for long periods of time, not because it *won't* buff later, but because it's very difficult to buff later because it gets so hard so quickly. The UFC-1 and the UFC-40 are excellent clears to buff, but the ideal time to buff those is within the first five to seven days of their completion. Many painters are buffing them in 48 hours and some in 24. We think 24 is the minimum time

Our UFC-40 Komply Klear is intended for the VOC sensitive areas. It is 52 percent solids ready to spray and uses the KU-400 catalyst. It's a beautiful, high-gloss clear. This is an excellent clear to buff, the ideal time is within the first five to seven days of completion. Many painters are buffing them in 48 hours and some in 24. We think 24 is the minimum time you should wait to buff to make sure that all of the solvents have left the clearcoat.

you should wait to buff to make sure that all of the solvents have left the clearcoat. There's no point in buffing something twice, because it's still drying. Ideally, 48 hours you're guaranteed you're going to get a good solid base.

Now we've come out with another clear for the most stringent requirements in California, and that's our UFC-80. It uses the KU-800 catalyst. This clear is 80 percent solids ready to spray. It does require that you use fewer coats because of its high solids content. One coat of this material is almost equivalent to three coats of the UC-1. You just don't need that many coats. The main problem we've had with the UFC-80 has been painters putting on the same number of coats as they have with other clears. It's not required. You basically can get

all the clear that you need in two coats.

A little reducer can be used, depending on your location. Northern California, for example, is not as stringent as southern California and some reducer can be added. It doesn't take very much reducer to make this a very, very nice clear to work with. This is our line up of clears. Each one has its own little idiosyncrasies on how it works. All of them have excellent pot life.

There are a few guidelines for using our clears. Don't mix your candy or your clear that contains catalyst until you're ready to use it. Some people down in the hot, humid climates - Louisiana, Texas - have gone ahead and mixed large quantities of this material hours before they're ready to paint, and when they

Our SG-100 is not a final clear. It is an intercoat clear designed as a protective clear for artwork and tapeouts on Shimrin bases. SG-100 prevents the tape from marking or pulling the metallic during tapeouts and allows clean up of mis-tapes. It may also be mixed with pearl and kandy koncentrates.

come back to do the painting, they've found that their material has turned to Jello. In high heat and high humidity conditions like this can easily happen.

Don't buy large quantities or containers of catalyst if you don't intend to use them up within a week or two. Once you break the seal on the catalyst can and you pour some out you eliminate the nitrogen blanket in that can. Once the blanket is poured out that product becomes sensitive to air in the can.

Most painters don't clean the threads of the can after they open it. Once you put a pliers to that cap you start losing your seal. Then the remaining catalyst will gain viscosity. They will get thicker and they will also pick up, unbeknownst to you, seeds that are very much like metallics. If you ever put an old catalyst into something and you spray it and it has an even pattern of "dirt" in it, you can look directly to your catalyst as being the culprit. Because it will pick up these clear seeds that will go through a strainer like metallic, but they'll show as dirt in the paint job.

Obviously, if the catalyst gains viscosity because it has absorbed moisture you're not going to get the same flow out. Your job is going to orange peel. So we highly recommend buying smaller quantities of the catalyst. In other words, instead of buying a gallon, buy four quarts. This is very important, because most other products have very long shelf lives, the

Our new Marblizers come in a variety of colors and can be used over and under other basecoats and kandies for an unlimited range of effects.

catalyst is one that does not.

On the safety side, remember that the catalyst is most dangerous when you're pouring it. You should protect yourself during pouring. Keep it off your skin. Don't breath it when it's a free monomer like this. When it mixes in the paint it becomes less hazardous, but then it's hazardous again when it's an airborne particle and you can ingest it in your respiratory system. Over long periods of painting, this can lodge in your organs and cause life-threatening things to take place.

Always wear the proper respirator. The TC19C is recommended. You don't want it on your skin. Wear eye protection, because it can enter your body through your eyes or any mucous membrane.

FINALLY

Before you pull the trigger, remember the most important points I've tried to make: Always walk the length of long objects, especially with a kandy or pearl because stopping in the middle of a panel, or a door edge will show up when the clear gets on. You will see the difference because every time the gun is stopped and started, the millage increases. In candies or pearls, this means you're going to be putting on more paint each time the gun is stopped and started. You don't need to do that. That means walking. We do it during the primer and during the sealer application. We just do this automatically.

For first time users, one of our videos might be a good way to minimize the anxiety of that first paint job. Just *call our tech line to order.*

Admittedly, some objects are very difficult to convert to a series of straight lines. For example, a Volkswagen Beetle. Every line converges. But it can be done and engineered to be painted properly. We love the tough-to-paint objects because it makes us think. We hope that we can get that through to you - that you pick a straight line and think. Measure things so you know what the

Good pinstriping requires a steady hand and plenty of practice. We typically scuff the surface to be pinstriped with 500 or 600 grit sandpaper so the clearcoat will adhere. This urethane enamel can be used catalyzed, or non-catalyzed if it will be topcoated.

Striping enamel: Our striping and Lettering Enamel is designed for striping, lettering and airbrush artwork. It feature high pigmentation, low solids for minimal edge and long open time. This paint can be applied over existing finishes or topcoated with lacquer or urethane.

taper is so that when you're making your moves you've got everything pre-planned and you know where you're going. Use common sense to ascertain how evenly you can apply the paint.

When applying a pearl and candy, remember to restrict the material and never the fan. Work in a close proximity with accurate pattern overlaps, with invisible straight lines drawn through the object, with a pass on the banding lines or any place that the panels turn.

The other rule is don't experiment on a large object. Always do a spray out on a panel to get more comfortable with the idea and to be sure everything is going to work. To make sure that your mix is right. It's wrong to experiment on something large. I learned that the hard way back in the early 1980s. I experimented with some new paint on my van and it wound up eating me alive. We painted that van four times, because the product should have been tested on something smaller. We all have to learn lessons by making mistakes, and that's unfortunate, but those are the lessons that seem to hang in our brain. Our goal in this book, in our tech manual and in our videos is to try to eliminate as many of these problems as we can so you don't have to go through the pain and misery that we have.

WHEN ALL ELSE FAILS....

I always tell painters to take the paint can into the lunch room and read the label instructions in a relaxed situation. Nobody is too smart that they don't have to read these label instructions. I don't care how long you've been painting. Particularly when you're working with our products for the first time. It's so important. Also request one of our tech books. They're given freely and there is so much information in there to help you understand the use of our products. A successful paint job requires that you understand how to use the products. Sometimes a picture is worth a thousand words. Seeing somebody do it in one of our videos can ease the pain or the anxiety of taking on a project like this.

Once you master this craft of custom painting, you will become a better painter no matter what products you're working with or how you're going about it because you have tuned and fine tuned yourself to be the violinist of the painting industry. You're not just an average painter that pumps out a standard finish. And as you can see, the finishes on the new cars are becoming more exotic each year. The man who is schooled in custom painting will handle these colors and touch ups like a breeze.

Our neons are designed to provide the ultimate in eye-grabbing brightness. These paints can be use as the final color with a topcoat of clear or as a base under a kandy color. Beware, however, these have limited light fastness in the sun.

Chapter Five

In The Shop: Basic Paint Jobs

Different paint jobs for different trucks

This chapter presents a hands-on view of two straightforward paint jobs. The first is a complete paint job on an Chevrolet S-10 Blazer. The second project seen here is a compete paint job on a 1985 Ford Pickup truck. Though the S-10 needed very little in the way of body work, the Ford required considerable body work and panel repair. Included in this chapter is a short discussion of the various paint stripping methods, and the advantages and disadvantages of each.

Stripped to the bare essentials in the plastic blasting booth, the S-10 displays a clean body that won't need much in the way of body work to get it ready for paint.

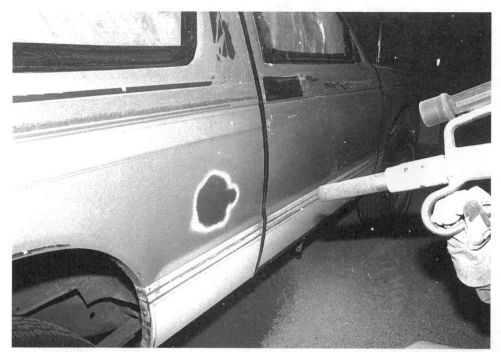

fying the dents we first took a thirty six grit pad on a grinder to rough up the low spots. With the metal prepared to accept the plastic filler we next mixed the filler thoroughly so as to distribute the hardener evenly. Then the filler was spread carefully over the dents in the S-10 body.

After the filler began to set up we began working the material with a mud hog (think of it as a DA sander with a more aggressive action) equipped with

Plastic blasting uses a low pressure stream of air carrying tiny bits of thermo-set plastic to strip the paint off the car with only minimal abrasion and almost no heat.

THE S-10

Before starting on the paint job for the S-10, the mini truck went to Precision Paint Removers in Long Lake, Minnesota so all the paint could be removed by the plastic blasting method. The crew at Precision Paint taped off the door openings and all the glass. With all the seams covered, they took all the paint off the body panels on the S-10.

While sand blasting uses a high pressure stream of sand to remove paint, plastic blasting uses a large volume of low pressure air (fifteen to forty psi) to propel very small thermo-set bits of plastic. The sharp edges on the plastic remove paint quickly but without the heat and abrasion that normally accompanies a sand blasting operation.

The plastic stripping took about two and a half hours. Most plastic blast operations charge by the minute, Kirby's charges $2.00 for each minute the gun runs. When you consider the mess and labor of chemically stripping the same vehicle, this seems pretty reasonable.

Once the car came into the House of Kolor shop, one of our technicians took on the job of getting the body ready for final paint. After identi-

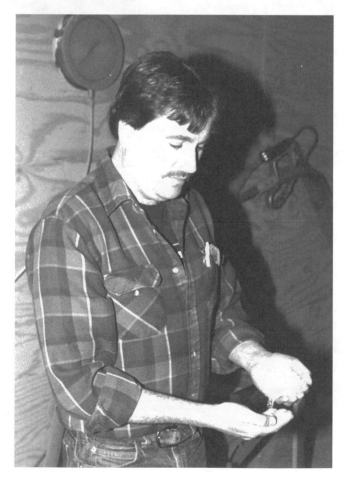

Kirby from Precision Paint Removers sifts a hand full of the thermo-set bits of plastic used to blast off the paint. Different grades of plastic are available, less aggressive material would be used with fiberglass bodies for example.

The S-10 required only one application of plastic filler. After sanding that first coat of filler Reuben applied a total of five coats of KP-2 primer (two on the filler and three more on the total truck). What looks like an uneven coat of paint is actually the guide coat Reuben put on before he starts block sanding.

Reuben goes through two block sanding sequences. First he sands with 80 and then 180. Low spots that show up are filled with polyester glaze. After block sanding the glaze and applying more KP-2, he block sands the truck again, this time with 280, then 400 grit (both wet).

a 36 grit pad. Once we had the filler in pretty good shape a DA sander with an 80 grit disc was used to feather the edges where the filler meets the steel and to knock the tops off the thirty six grit scratches. Next we went over the entire car with a 240 grit pad on the DA sander. Because there weren't any big dents in the little truck, only one coat of plastic filler was needed.

The next step is the application of primer. For this job we chose to use our KP-2, Kwikure Epoxy Primer. Per the instructions, we mixed equal amounts of part A and B and began applying the primer to the areas covered in plastic filler first. Two coats are applied to the areas that received body work, allowing the KP-2 to flash between coats (the KP-2 has flashed when it looses its gloss and goes dull). Then an additional three coats are applied to the rest of the S- 10.

After allowing the primer to cure for 24 hours we apply a guide coat (a light dusting of dark lacquer primer that will highlight the low spots) and begin block sanding with eighty grit paper. From eighty we move to 180 grit and eventually block sand the entire car. The inevitable low spots, which show up dark due to the remaining guide coat, are scratched with eighty grit and then filled with two-part polyester gaze. Lighter than filler and heavier than primer-surfacer, the glaze can be applied over paint as a quick means of filling low spots that show up after the basic body work is done (plastic filler should only be applied over bare metal, an earlier coat of filler or primer that has been roughened with 80 grit).

The glaze sets up quickly allowing us to block sand the glaze with 80 and then 180 grit paper on a sanding block. Once the glaze is level with the surrounding areas it's time for another application of primer. And for this we first apply two coats of the KP-2 to areas

After the roof is painted then Denny moves onto the side panels, doing the edges first.

Denny starts the final painting with a coat of Ko-seal 903, dark gray. Note the pattern, first he paints the windshield posts and edges of the roof.

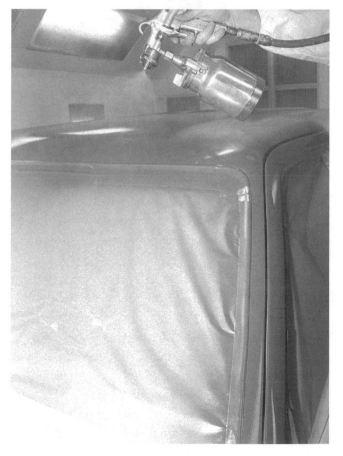

Next he paints the roof, keeping the gun parallel to the panel, moving in straight lines (easier with rectangular panels). Each new pass overlaps the last one by 50%.

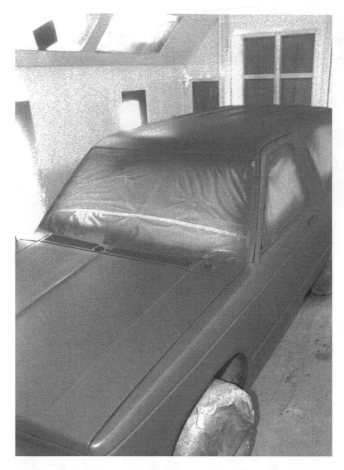

The sealer aids adhesion of the topcoat and promotes good color holdout - the most important thing sealer does is make the car one uniform color, hopefully something close to the final color.

that were glazed and then an additional two coats to the entire vehicle (allowing for the material to flash between coats). When the KP-2 has cured for 24 hours. We block sand the truck with 280 and then 400 grit, keeping the paper wet during the process.

A few more small low spots show up so we do one more application of polyester glaze, which is allowed to dry and then coated with two coats of KP-2. After the required 14 hour wait, the areas most recently glazed are block sanded with 400 grit paper.

Then we wash the car down with soapy water followed by a rinse. Any areas that seem to repel the soapy water are assumed to be contaminated with oil from someone's hands and washed again or scuffed with 400 grit paper. Then the car is wiped down with final wash on a clean rag.

Our Ko-seal is thinned at the standard ratio of one part sealer to one and one half parts thinner (we used 202 in this case) and applied to the entire car. Part of the reason for using sealer is to create a uniform color, close to the final paint color, and thus obtain faster coverage with the final color. Ko-seal 903, dark gray is the color we applied in one medium coat, which is allowed to dry 30 to 60 minutes and not sanded.

The next step is three medium coats (in some cases two would be adequate) of BC-25 black, the base coat for the kandy which will follow. We apply the three coats fairly quickly (this material acts like a lacquer and dries fast) and run a tack rag over the car before I begin to apply the kandy coats.

The topcoat for the truck is our new Kandy Base Coat, number KBC-04, oriental blue. These

Here we apply the black basecoat to the roof. The driver's side of the roof is done first and then we move over to the other side of the car. Three coats of basecoat are applied before we switch to the Kandy Base Coat oriental blue.

new paints are reduced with our RU-series reducers but are not catalyzed. I put on three coats of the new product with my DeVilbiss siphon-style high-pressure gun, (though an HVLP gun could have been used) waiting for flash times between each coat. After the third coat has flashed I darken the lower body panels and body line in the hood by applying another two coats of KBC-05 cobalt blue, to the lower

Any areas that seem to repel the soapy water are assumed to be contaminated with oil from someone's hands and washed again or scuffed with 400 grit paper.

panels and along the body line in the hood.

For the clearcoat on this truck we choose our UFC-1, which I put on in three coats. And because there is virtually no dust in the finished paint (we were careful to wear a painter's suit and keep the booth clean) there is no need to polish the paint on the S-10. All that's left is to put the hardware back on the body.

THE FORD PICKUP

The pickup truck seen here is one of the House of Kolor shop trucks. After hav-

After putting three coats of the KBC oriental blue on the truck, I blend in some KBC cobalt blue on the lower body panel and also on the hood.

The finished truck waiting for final clean up. The clearcoat is three coats of UFC-1 with no color sanding or polishing.

Paint Stripping

As I've said before, "In order to get longevity on a custom paint job, we feel that it should be the only paint job on the vehicle."

There are a variety of ways to remove the paint that's already on the vehicle though none of them are easy or cheap. Methods that work well for small parts don't always lend themselves to complete bodies. Stripping processes that take off paint don't necessarily remove rust.

The stripping methods break down into four basic processes: blasting, dipping, chemical stripping and sanding. Here's a short look at each one.

BLASTING

The best known blasting technique is sand blasting, definitely an aggressive method of paint removal. Though this mechanical process may work well for large, heavy objects like frame rails, there are some problems when sand blasting is used on sheet metal. First, the stream of sand propelled by high pressure air hits the sheet metal with tremendous force and that force and abrasion creates heat.

Second, the pits created by the sand blasting stretch the metal causing more warpage. If that weren't enough, the heat causes embrittlement of the steel. So while we use a small sandblaster in our shop for a section of the body (like the edges of the quarter panels on our Ford truck), it's not a good idea to sand blast an entire body unless the pressure is turned down and the operator is careful.

Plastic blasting is a relatively new process. Less aggressive than sand blasting, this process can be used to remove paint without attacking and warping the metal itself. The particles themselves are made from thermoset plastic, each particle has sharp edges designed to cut paint without the need for high air pressure.

The length of time it takes to strip a part or a body depends on its size, the type of paint and the number of paint layers. Kirby, owner and operator of Precision Paint Removers, explained that "We charge two dollars per minute that the gun runs. The S-10 was fairly easy because the paint was sun faded and bleached, but a body of that size typically takes two and a half hours or a little more."

The plastic stripping process is so delicate that a good operator can actually take the paint off one layer at a time. In fact, it's so gentle that any old filler - or rust - that shows up under the paint will be left intact. The equipment runs on a high volume of relatively low-pressure air - twenty to forty pounds. The media is recycled, filtered and used over again, until it gets too pulverized to cut the paint. In fact, new media is seldom used alone, some old media is usually mixed with the

Once the old paint is removed the parts are placed in baskets and immersed in the solution. The D.C. electricity, run between the body and the solution, causes the ions which float free in the solution to bond with the rust, thereby breaking the chemical bonds that hold the rust molecules together.

new in order to dampen the cutting action. Because the old media and paint dust contains no toxic chemicals disposal of the dust is never a problem and helps to hold down the cost.

Kirby feels the price of plastic blasting is quite competitive, explaining, "If you look at how much it costs to strip a body with chemical stripper the old way, this is usually faster, cheaper and doesn't make that incredible mess."

Precision Paint Removers is located in Long Lake Minnesota, west of Minneapolis. In other parts of the country a shop can be located by calling the Dry Stripping Facilities Network (DSFN-an industry group). They will direct you to the nearest dry stripping specialist. See the Sources section for the phone number of Precision Paint Removers and the DSFN.

DIP STRIPPING

If you can't eliminate the rust with plastic blasting, what can you do to get the rust off that old body? Dip stripping might be the answer. This type of stripping, where the entire body or basket of parts is lowered into a bath of some kind, breaks down into two very different methods: acid dipping and electrochemical stripping.

ACID DIPPING

Acid dipping is just what the name implies, an acid bath for your rusty parts. The acid removes rust but it also removes some of the good metal as well. Thus it becomes dangerous to take in the door from the Model A with the rust perforation along the bottom edge - as there might not be much door skin left when it comes out of the bath. The other problem with the acid dip is the effect of residual acid, left behind in pinch welds and crevices, on new paint. Another potential problem is the fact that the acid can cause embrittlement of the steel making it harder to work that metal later.

A better dip strip method involves a non-acid bath, known as electrochemical or electrolytic cleaning. This non-corrosive process removes paint and rust without attacking any of the good metal.

ELECTROCHEMICAL DIPPING

Electrochemical cleaning is a process that removes the rust, all the rust and only the rust from that old body. Holes that were the size of a quarter when you brought the body in will be exactly the same size when you take the body home. The only difference is that the rust around that hole will be gone completely.

Before the rust can be removed, most electrochemical strippers first take off the old paint. Some facilities strip the paint off with a caustic bath followed by a high pressure spray, while others use plastic blasting to strip off the paint.

Once the old paint is removed, the parts are placed in baskets and immersed in an alkaline solution. Once in the solution, a DC current is run between the body and the solution. The electricity causes the ions which float

Though large sand blasters can do great damage to sheet metal parts, a small blaster can be used to get the rust out of small areas without creating too much heat and abrasion.

Large objects like car bodies are suspended on special fixtures and kept in the solution for as long as it takes to get all the rust off - and what took years and years to form may take at least days and days to dissolve.

take the time to dispose of them responsibly. Each brand of stripper will have a different set of directions - be sure to take the time to read them. Most recommend that you score the surface with a razor blade for example, to help the stripper get under the surface of the paint and work faster.

Most can be brushed on with an old paint brush. By moving the brush in only one direction the material will "glaze over" because of the paraffin in the stripper comes to the top. This prevents it from drying out and keeps the stripper working below that glazed surface. If you brush back and forth this anti-drying agent is rendered useless.

The paint stripper works best if you give it time to work. You will probably need to scrape off the softened paint and put on more stripper. Two or three applications are often necessary and will still require some hand work with sand paper at edges and crevices after the stripper is all removed. Be sure to tape off openings and body seams so the material will not enter those areas. Final wash thoroughly with water or a cleanser like acetone.

free in the solution to bond with the rust, thereby breaking the chemical bonds that hold the rust molecule together. Chemically, rust is just iron oxide. Once the bond is broken the iron remains in suspension and the oxygen floats to the surface. The unrusted steel is unaffected by this process.

All this chemical bonding and de-bonding takes time, so the process isn't quick or cheap. Typical immersion times range from overnight for light rust, to three or four days for heavy accumulations of rust. Though it isn't cheap, electrochemical cleaning is the best, most thorough cleaning method for rusty parts. Precision Paint Removers is due to open an electro chemical stripping operation soon. And there are ads in *Hemmings* for other operations in different parts of the country.

CHEMICAL STRIPPING

A variety of paint strippers are available at the hardware or paint supply store. Most will remove nearly any type of paint. This process is not easy, even on small parts and requires rubber gloves, an apron, safety glasses and good ventilation.

Most of the strippers qualify as toxic waste (check the labels, some are designed to be nontoxic). If you use much of the materials you should

SANDING

Sanding is a popular means of removing paint because everyone has a grinder and it works reasonably well if the parts aren't too big. But remember that grinders add a lot of heat to the sheet metal which can work-harden the metal. Also, you can't use too coarse a grit on the thin, tempered steel found on the new cars.

If you're going to add plastic filler to the area where you're grinding then you may want some deep sanding marks to give the filler something to stick to. But if all you're doing is taking off the paint, try to use a smaller grinder and a finer grit pad - it will save you work in the long run.

ing a modified big-block engine installed it seemed appropriate to eliminate the rust that was starting to eat away at the fenders on our Minnesota 4X4 and give the truck a compete paint job.

We start the job at the back of the truck where rust has perforated the edges of the rear quarter panels. Patch panels are ordered for the quarters, but rather than install the entire panel we trim the panel to cover only

---

It is very important to blend the filler and hardener very thoroughly so you don't end up with air bubbles in the filler or with areas in the filler that never set-up

---

the rusty edge. Before welding the panel to the fender, we sand blast and grind most of the rust off the fender edge. Next while one of us holds the panel in place, another clamps it and then starts the welding with the wire feed welder.

After the panels are welded in place we sand blasts all the lingering rust at the edge of the fender again and also eliminate any oxidation at the weld bead. Before applying the plastic filler to the fender edge, the area is ground with a grinder

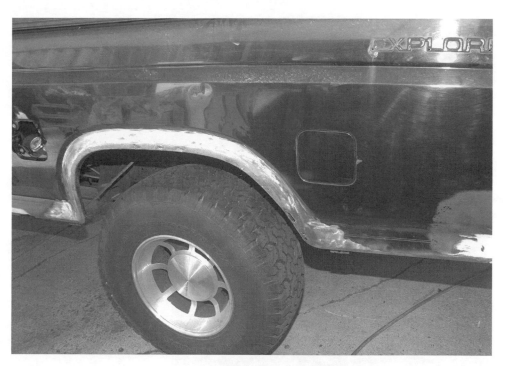

Here we see the "before" picture of the rear fender. rusty perforations at the edge will be ground clean and then covered with a patch panel.

Reuben holds the patch panel - which has been trimmed to the bare minimum - up against the old fender.

Before welding the patch panel in place a specialized grinding disc is used to grind off as much rust as possible.

First the patch panel is clamped in place and then a wire-feed welder is used to weld it to the old fender.

equipped with a 36 grit pad so the filler is sure to have something to grab onto.

Now it's time for plastic filler, which is mixed according to the instructions. It is very important to blend the filler and hardener very thoroughly so you don't end up with air bubbles in the filler or with areas in the filler that never set-up because there is no hardener at that spot. Note, the plastic filler will absorb moisture that might come through the backside of the patch panes or weld bead, so we mix up some epoxy and use that to seal up the backside of the fender lip. This will also help to eliminate rust problems in the future.

The first coat of filler is applied to the weld bead and then to the entire patch area. The filler goes on in a series of applications. It's a hot day when we do this and the filler sets up fast. Because of this we mix small batches and put them on quickly before mixing more filler.

The filler is mixed on a plastic panel though we often mix it on cardboard. They say not to use cardboard but with a fresh piece of cardboard I know I'm not getting any old pieces of filler in the new batch I'm mixing (and I mix and use it fast so the resin does not soak into the cardboard). The initial shaping or first

Reuben applied the plastic filler carefully, applying only as much as he needs. The filler is mixed on a plastic panel, though we often use cardboard. It's important to push it down firmly to minimize air bubbles in the filler - which then have to be filled later.

coat of plastic filler is done with a mud hog equipped with 40 grit paper. (We have a smaller size mud hog too for areas you can't reach with the big unit.)

Usually you can finish the filler and do your repair with two coats of filler - especially if you do a lot of mud work. If you don't do much mud work though, it might take three coats. My job has always been to get the job done, do it right and get it out of the shop. So I work in 40 grit for both the first and second coat, then block sand by hand in 40 or 80. I never go finer than 80 grit on the filler and only use enough 80 to take out the worst of the 40 grit scratches.

In the case of our truck, we mix and apply a third coat of filler for the remaining low spots along the fender edge. This third coat is sanded with 40 grit on the smaller mud hog, because it is lighter and easier to get into the recesses in the panels.

As we work on the truck we discover a few dents that should be pulled instead of just filled with plastic. We use the stud gun system for pulling dents, which consists of a mini spot welder, specialized studs and a slide hammer. This system is nice as it gives you something to grab onto without drilling

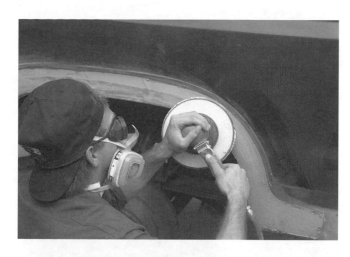

A mud hog with 40 grit paper is used to shape the first coat of filler.

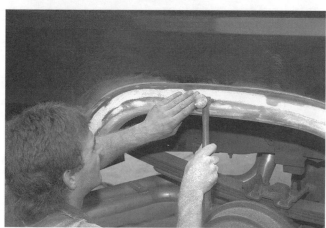

High spots of metal often show up at this point, and Reuben gently knocks one down with the body hammer.

When the first coat is shaped and the high points knocked down, it's time for the second coat of plastic filler, applied carefully so it needs as little shaping as possible. The fender edges will eventually get one more coat of plastic filler before they are primered.

After grinding away the paint, Reuben uses the specialized spot welder (part of the Dent-Fix system) to weld a copper stud to the lowest part of the dent in the body panel.

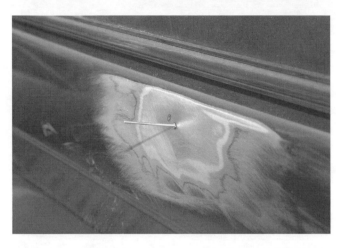

The system leaves the copper stud welded to the panel, and the next step is....

holes in the panel. The process breaks down to a few simple steps:

1. Find the low spot and remove the paint.
2. Spot weld a specialized copper stud to the center of the low spot.
3. Attach the slide hammer to the stud.
4. Pull out the dent with blows from the slide hammer.
5. Grind off the stud and prepare the area for filler.
6. Apply filler as you would any other body repair.

After finishing the fender lip and the other small dents on the quarter panel with the small mud hog and 40 grit paper we use a long sanding block equipped with 80 grit paper and start in with block sanding by hand. It's important to note that the block sanding is nearly always done in a cross hatch or "X" pattern because the paper cuts faster that way and also because that way you avoid sanding flat spots into the panel - which helps maintain the curvature found in most modern automotive panels.

After knocking down the 40 grit sanding scratches with the 80 grit paper, we spray a guide coat (dark lacquer primer) and then do more block sanding with 80 grit. The dark paint makes the low spots easy to see. These low spots will be filled with some polyester

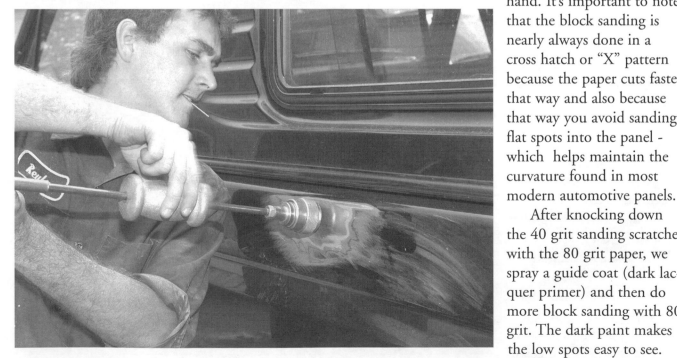

A few blows from the slide hammer, then grind off the stud, add a coat of filler and then finish like you would any other damaged area.

glaze and block sanded again with more 80 grit.

After we're happy with the basic condition of the rear quarter panels we blow off all the dust and wipe the truck off with a good a final wash product that leaves no oily residues. Next comes the KP-2 two-part primer. The primer is applied in five coats in the following sequence: One coat on the body work. One coat on the complete panel. One more on the body work, then the second and third complete panel applications. Each coat is allowed to flash before we apply another.

After allowing the KP-2 to fully cure for 24 hours (at a minimum of 70 degrees), another guide coat is applied before the block sanding begins. Then we start with 80 grit paper on a sanding pad before we move to a 180 grit pad. The idea at this point is to fill the 36 and 80 grit scratches. Low spots that show up at this stage are filled with the two-part polyester glazing putty, then block sanded wet with 400 grit.

After all the obvious low spots are filled with glaze and block sanded it's time for another two coats of KP-2. After the 14 hour cure time we again apply a guide coat but now we move to 400 grit paper on

When all the dents in the quarter panel have been filled with filler and finished to Reuben's satisfaction, he washes and wipes down the fender before applying five coats of KP-2. The KP-2 is allowed to cure for 24 hours before block sanding with 80 and then 180 grit paper.

Here we sand off the guide coat, following the rule to always block sand in an X pattern to avoid sanding flat spots and ridges in the panels. This is the second round of block sanding and any low spots that we find will be filled with polyester glaze.

This low spot on the lower panel is a prime candidate for a thin layer of glazing putty.

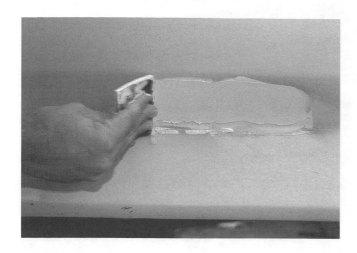

A small rubber pad is used to apply and shape the two-part polyester glaze, which sets up very quickly.

After only a short wait we go back in and block sand the area Then we apply another two coats of primer, allow that to cure, and then do the final block sanding to this area.

Sometimes called spot putty, we use only a high quality two-part polyester glaze for low spots that don't require plastic filler. Like plastic filler, it is important to use the recipe on the can and mix it thoroughly so the two parts are thoroughly blended.

a sanding block (we recommend that you use 320 to 400 grit paper, never finer, as the final sanding grit before sealer is applied).

The front fenders are too far gone to repair so we put on two new ones. Before hanging the new fenders on the truck we take the DA, equipped with 240 grit paper, to the outside of the fender, then scuff the inside with 240 grit dry. After wiping down the fender we apply two coats of UB-4 black on the inside and the edges of the fender.

Using the hood as a guide, we hang the fenders, and then later a new hood as well (the hood was painted on the inside just like the fenders). The new panels don't have many dents so we prepare them with three coats of KP 2, then we block sand with 400 grit wet.

The door skins on our truck are in good shape, but there were a few small dings. We didn't want to grind down to bare metal as is necessary for the application of plastic filler, so after going over the panels with a DA and 240 grit paper we used one application of polyester glazing putty in the low spots. Then the glazed areas are block sanded with 80 and finally 150 grit paper. After wiping the doors down with final wash and a tack rag we apply one coat of KP-2 to areas that were filled with glaze. After that first coat of KP-2 has flashed, the entire door skins get another two coats of our primer-surfacer. When the KP-2 has cured fully it's time for a guide coat and block sanding with 180 grit. Before applying sealer we apply another three coats of KP-2 before doing the final block sanding with wet, 400 grit paper.

It's interesting to note the extra care that we took with this job and how that helps produce a quality job. To bring the big 4X4 closer to the ground during the painting we took the wheels off and set it on jack stands. And to make it easy to paint the back of the cab and the roof we unbolted the box and slid it back off the frame. Of course we removed the bumpers and trim so we could get in and do a quality job. We also used the Folex system to pull the rubbers away from the sheet metal before applying the final paint.

When the entire truck has been repaired and block sanded as described we apply one coat of Ko-seal. Because the final color will be black, we cover the entire truck with KO 903 dark grey sealer.

The final paint is UFB-4 black (we use the right

At this point the new front fenders are mounted (after we painted the back side). The doors have been sanded, any small dings will be filled with glaze before we coat the door skins with KP-2 primer.

In the booth, we pull the wheels off the truck to get it down to a height that makes it easier to paint. The next step is to wipe it down and apply one coat of Ko-seal.

Our truck in the booth after three coats of UFB-4 black. We still have to color sand the black (you can see we have already started on the back of the cab) and then do the final "clearcoat." The clearcoat in this case is UFB-4 mixed 50/50 with clear, with extra reducer.

The color sanding is done with 500 grit paper on a variety of sanding blocks, keeping the paper wet as we work. This will flatten the black paint and increase the total shine.

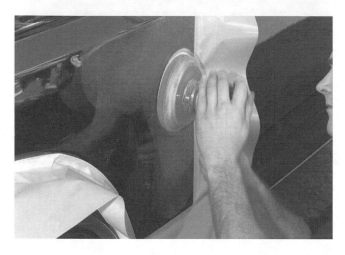

Our polishing of the truck starts with a special 1000 grit "interface" pad from 3M on the DA.

The 3M system includes the special sanding pads, as well as wool and foam pads for the electric buffer and different grades of cutting and polishing liquids for the different buffing pads.

reducer for the booth temperature and KU500 catalyst) applied in one medium and two wet coats with flash time between each coat.

Twelve hours after painting we color sand the entire truck with 500 grit paper on a sanding block except for curves where it is done by hand. We use different sanding blocks for different areas and stay away from body lines and creases where it is easy to sand through. The water keeps the paper from plugging up and helps flush away the sanding debris.

We put enough paint on the truck (probably four mils) that we can sand off one mil with no danger of sanding through. This wet color sanding will flatten the paint and add to the eventual shine. By applying our flowcoats within 24 hours of the final coat of black they will bond chemically with the black.

After color sanding the black, I apply three coats of UFC-1 clearcoat and UFB-4 mixed one to one. Again this is reduced, catalyzed with the KU-500(not the KU-100) and then we wait a full 24 hours before the start of color sanding and polishing.

POLISHING AND COLOR SANDING

We start by masking off one fender so the compound doesn't get into the grill and areas where it will just make a mess and be hard to clean up. The system used for the truck is the 3M system (though the Mequiar's products work well too).

We start with a 1000 grit 3M interface pad on the DA and go over the fender with that. Body lines and creases are taped off so there is no chance to sand through the paint at an edge.

After finishing with the DA we go to a soft sanding pad and some 1200-1500 grit paper which we keep wet as we work. The next step will be 2000 grit and then polishing with our power buffer which operates at a maximum of 1500 RPM.

The first pad on the power buffer is a wool pad and the 05711 liquid Perfect-It II Rubbing Compound. Once again, it's important to avoid the edges as we work. The next step is a 3M diamond-shaped foam finish pad and some Perfect-It Foam Polishing Pad Glaze. Before putting away the power buffer there is one more step with the Finesse-It II Finishing material. After all that work with power tools, the final step is Hand Glaze applied with a soft cotton towel. When we're done the black fender truly looks like glass.

Near the end of the sequence we're working with the foam pad and the liquid finishing material. Each step further polishes the paint and eliminates scratches left by the last step.

After all that work and TLC we've created one very nice looking truck. For a great paint job you need quality materials used according to the directions. You also need the patience to finish each step correctly before rushing into the next one.

Chapter Six

In The Shop: Beyond Basic Paint

Trick paint for two wheels and four

This chapter covers two paint jobs that go considerably beyond basic. The Sportster is a candy paint job that illustrates how to use our kandy urethanes and the kandy koncentrates as well. Of note, we don't just paint the sheet metal, but the wheels (cast aluminum) as well.

The second paint job in this chapter is a rather complex job done to the Dragster which belongs to Mike Stevens one of our employees. The dragster paint job, because of the complexity, illustrates

Here we see the finished gas tank, after all the basecoats, kandycoats, graphics and clearcoats have been applied.

a variety of art work and painting techniques.

Keep in mind the fact that the essential painting techniques are the same, whether the vehicle being painted has two wheels or four (or six!). Don't ignore one of the motorcycle painting sequences just because your plans are to paint a car - the paint doesn't know the difference.

THE SPORTSTER

The motorcycle sheet metal seen here is all part of custom Harley-Davidson Sportster project owned by Patty Crandall and assembled by Bill Messenbrink, both from Minneapolis.

As we've said before, a good foundation is as important to a custom paint job as it is in building a house. For this motorcycle application we apply two coats of KP-2 to areas that have received body work and then another three coats to the entire surface, allowing for adequate flash time between coats.

The wheels are next to receive primer. To dress up the bike Patty has chosen to paint the factory cast wheels. Because they are polished at the edges we had to carefully wipe the whole wheel down with acetone (remember that acetone and similar solvents are very flammable) to be sure we removed all the polishing rouge from the corners, edges and rough-cast parts of the wheel.

Because they both contain zinc chromate, either

The design of the graphics are taped out free-hand, after scuffing the clearcoats we laid down over the kandy. I never use a grease pencil to mark out the design but just start working with the eighth inch tape.

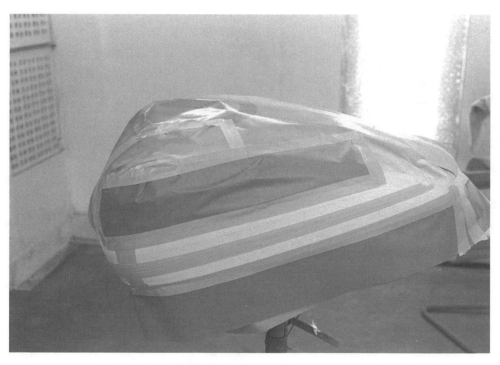

Because we need a white basecoat under the graphics, we tape out the entire design, then apply the white basecoat. After allowing the basecoat to dry it's time to apply tape to everything but the two stripes near the bottom of the tank.

A touch up gun is used to apply the Shimrin Designer Pearls. These paints act like lacquers, they go on and dry fast allowing us to move quickly through a job like this.

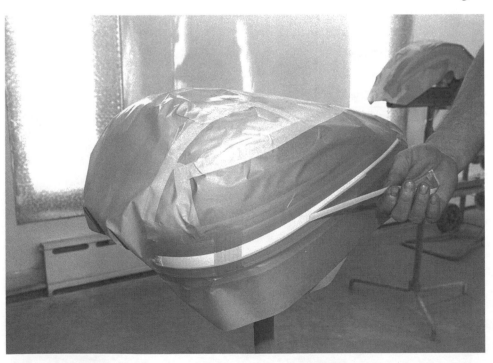

After the two, sunrise pearl and tangelo, stripes are painted we reverse tape and pull the tape for the center stripe.

the EP-2 or KP-2 can be used to prime the cast aluminum wheels. We chose to use a single coat of KP-2 as primer (with no sealer used) for the wheels.

The next step is to seal the sheet metal parts. Koseal KO 901 is applied to the sheet metal and frame. The 901 is the light grey color, chosen to work with the blue that will be used for the base color.

After applying the Koseal, we wait one hour (never more than two hours or you must sand and reshoot the sealer) and then begin application of the base coat.

The basecoat is metallic blue BC-04, one of our Shimrin basecoats, applied in three medium coats. The kandy color will be UK-4 kandy oriental blue. Shooting blue over blue it's real hard to make a mistake. I always tell people to do it that way if they're starting out. Putting on the basecoat is usually pretty easy, the hard part is the kandy application. By applying blue over blue any little differences in coverage that happen as you spray the kandy are much less obvious than they would be if the blue were applied over a lighter color base.

We put on four coats of the UK-4 kandy after allowing the final basecoat to dry for thirty minutes (never let the Shimrin basecoats sit more than one hour before being topcoated, unless you clear them with SG-100 for later sanding or artwork). The kandy is applied in two medium and two wet coats with flash times between each coat.

For the wheels, we started with three coats of basecoat just like the sheet metal. Objects like wheels, with an unusual shape, can be hard to paint and hard to paint evenly. In order to avoid having to put five or six coats of kandy on the wheels and maybe get uneven coverage, I add some of our kandy koncentrate (KK series additive) to the oriental blue kandy. By using the koncentrate to strengthen the kandy we were able to get good coverage and color in only two applications of the oriental blue with a final clearcoat.

Here you can see the three stripes along the bottom of the tank, with the tape pulled on the arc.

GRAPHICS AND COLOR SANDING

After the paint on the sheet metal has dried for a minimum of 12 hours we knock down the shine by sanding with 500 (never finer than 600 or it hurts the adhesion of the next coat) grit paper. People worry about the scratches but the first coat of clear will fill those 500 grit scratches with ease. We use plenty of water, we like to use ivory liquid dish detergent in the water (in limited amounts) to help keep the paper from plugging up with sanding debris.

When it comes to graphics, it's OK to do art work over our Kandies - as long as you apply a clearcoat first to prevent bleeding -

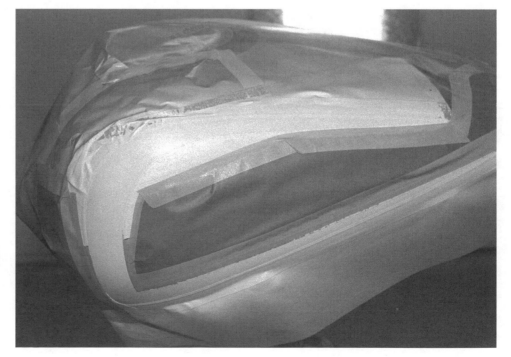

Next we tape off those lower stripes, leaving only the arc exposed and ready for the next color.

This is the tank following all the graphics, the clearcoat of the whole tank and the pinstriping. The tank is dull because we haven't applied the clearcoats.

Here's the finished product. The "final" clearcoats are done in two stages. First we apply three coats, then we sand those to eliminate any ridge over the pinstripes. Then we apply three more clearcoats and do the final polishing.

using our Shimrin bases. I recommend the Shimrins because they're low solids so you only get a minimum film build. When you're doing this, use a fast drying reducer. (Shimrins use no catalyst) as fast as you can use in your conditions. The 311 has extra tail solvents, you don't use it in this application unless it's real, hot, like in Texas. Use 310 or a mix of 310 and 311, never 312. The 310 works up to 80 or 85 degrees, hold the gun close and spray light to medium coats. Never spray Shimrins wet and heavy, especially as artwork over a catalyzed urethane.

Allow a good wait between coats, so you don't trap solvents. It's easy to trap solvents here especially on the last coat. Remember, the Shimrin bases are lacquer-like in their behavior, so the waits aren't long. I should mention that problems with lifting can almost always be traced to using 311 or 312 instead of 310 reducer, or to trapping solvents by ignoring the flash times.

For the design of the graphics I tape it out freehand, based on an idea in a magazine that the customer likes.

I always recommend to people that they go out and buy eighth inch crepe tape from 3M and just start playing. I've seen guys who start with chalk and draw out the design and all that, but that's not the best way to do it. Just get some tape and do it until you like what you've done.

The design consists of a series of color bands along the bottom of the tank and an arch of color that runs from the front of the tank to the back. We tape off the entire tank except those areas that will make up the new design. A white basecoat will be applied to all the areas that make up the design, but before applying the white base coat we tack the area. The three coats of BC-26 white are applied in three light coats using number 310 as the reducer, with a wait of three to five minutes between coats (use a touch test to be sure the paint has flashed before applying the next coat).

After allowing the final basecoat to dry for approximately a half hour we tape off everything but two horizontal stripes along the bottom of the tank. Then we shoot the first color, (all are Shimrin Designer Pearls) PBC 30 sunrise pearl. These are low-solids paints and we put the paint on in 3 light coats. The idea is to get complete coverage with minimum film build so you don't have trouble burying the edges later. With the touch up gun running on 35 psi we are able to put the yellow on the bottom stripe, without completely masking off the upper stripe, because there is very little over spray. We always recommend putting the lighter color on first, followed by the darker second color on the upper stripe.

Next, we spray the PBC-32 tangelo on the upper stripe allowing some overspray to darken the yellow on the lower stripe. When both colors are applied and dried, we put on one coat of SG-100 inter-coat clear. This is done to protect the pearl basecoats. It's also necessary because it will be more than one hour (the correct window of time for topcoating the Shimrin pearls) before we can come in with the next coat of paint. With the SG-100 we can scuff the clear, not the pearl, which is always a no-no. The SG-100 is reduced 50 percent, with number RU-310 reducer. Of note, the SG-100 is not intended as a final clearcoat (there are other uses for SG-100, however, which can be found in the tech book).

After the SG-100 is dry (roughly one hour depending on shop conditions) we pull the tape in the center, between the two stripes and "reverse tape" the area, so we can do a hot pink stripe between the other two bands of color. When we reverse tape it is important to leave a little orange showing at the edge of the tape so we don't have white stripe showing when we're through. The center stripe is done with two coats of PBC 35 pink pearl and then fogged with hot pink pearl number PBC-39.

The fogging is done by eye with the gun adjusted down to a "dot" pattern. Then we put on one coat of SG-100 and then pull the paper and uncover the arc we taped off earlier. Next we reverse tape the orange , yellow, pink stripes, then spray the big arc. To be good at doing art work and tape outs you have to know exactly what to tape in what sequence. Think before you paint, it will save you time.

After the next round of reverse taping I spray 3 coats of PBC- 65 passion pearl. Next we decide to highlight the passion with PBC 40 violet pearl. Because this purple arch is the last color and because we are going to apply the next coat of clear (to the entire tank) within one hour, we do not spray SG-100 over the purple, but instead pull the tape off the tank and then prepare to apply the clearcoat (UC-1 in this case) to the entire tank. Before clearcoating I often take a dull picket knife to the edges where they met the tape to knock down the high points.

After pulling the tape we scuff the whole thing with a grey scotch-brite pad and soapy water. This is a good time to correct little mis-tapes. I always like to watch for places where the water separates from the tank. Because if the water jumps off the paint won't go there either. Then wipe it down with a clean rag, blow it off with a blow gun so no water is lurking under the gas cap recess for example, and then do the final tack prior to application of the clear.

Then the UC-1 is applied in three coats, one bond coat and two wet coats. After the final clearcoat is dried for a minimum of 12 hours at 70 degrees we sand the tank with 500 grit paper wet. The next step is to the pinstriper's shop and then it comes back for the final clearcoats.

PINSTRIPES

For pinstriping the motorcycle parts go to pinstripe artist, D.J. Eckel in Minneapolis. D.J. uses a Mack brush with natural bristles. The brushes come in various sizes from 00 or 000 (the smallest) to a number 5 or more. The 00, is Dave's favorite. These brushes are available at art supply or auto body supply stores.

The paint is our urethane sign painting paint, which is designed to be clearcoated, unlike some of

This is the number 12 pounce wheel, used to perforate the paper that will be used to transfer the logo to both sides of the car.

To place the House of Kolor Logo on the side of the car, a small copy of the logo is enlarged onto a piece of paper, and then the outlines are all gone over with a pounce wheel, leaving small perforations in the paper.

the other sign painting enamels like One Shot. Because we're applying pinstripes over a cured catalyzed urethane mistakes can be easily wiped off with acetone without damaging the paint underneath.

Dave uses our color card to find the right colors for the pinstripes by holding various colors up against the Sportster tank until he finds a combination of colors that work together.

Dave "pallets" the brush across a piece of glossy paper or light board. This action forces paint up into the heel of the brush and allows you to pull a longer line. This also lets the painter feel how thick the paint is. The paint must have the right consistency (just the right amount of thinner) in order to have definition and not leave any uneven stripes.

COLOR SANDING

After the pinstriping we clean the tank and fenders with soapy water and a grey Scotch Brite pad. It is essential to get the parts clean and wipe them off with clean rags to get off all the oily fingerprints. Then we blow it off, tack the tank and apply three wet coats of clear. The final clearcoats are UFC-1 applied in a "flow coat," with extra

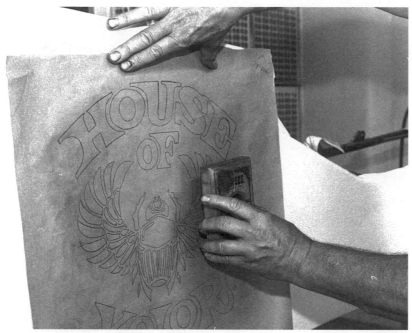

be surrounded in black for maximum contrast, though the letters and the beetle will be done in kandies and for those we want the white pearl basecoat. The white pearl basecoat is scuffed with a grey scotch brite pad before going any further.

For a pattern we take the House of Kolor logo and enlarge it onto a piece of light paper. After checking the enlargement we lay the piece of paper with the enlarged logo on some rags and go over the outlines of

Here you can see the "pounced" outline of the logo taped to the car while the pounce pad is taped against the car. The dark chalk in the pad will transfer through the holes, leaving an imprint of the logo.

reducer. Though the UFC-1 doesn't require polishing (except to remove dirt or for extreme flatness) we do color sand and polish the tanks using the Meguiar's system described in another chapter of this book.

MIKE'S DRAGSTER

Note: most of the shop projects in this book are described in exactly the sequence in which they were prepared and painted. Because two and three people worked on this dragster at one time we have broken the project down into smaller "sub-projects." So you will read about how we did the House of Kolor logo, the colored panels on the side and the long stripes on the nose.

But first we prepared the entire car with three coats of EP-2 epoxy primer (we had plenty of time to let the car sit and cure) then one coat of Ko-seal, then the BC-26 white base was applied to the entire car in three medium coats with 50 percent pattern overlap.

THE HOUSE OF KOLOR LOGO

First I position the logo by drawing out a big circle on the side of the car with a big protractor and a stabilo pencil. The House of Kolor logo will

The chalk leaves a faint outline which is then used as a guide to mask out the logo.

the design with a number 12 pounce wheel. The pounce wheel cuts little holes in the paper, but before using the paper as a pattern we scuff the back side with 280 grit nofil dry sanding paper to open up the holes and eliminate the small paper tabs.

Next we tape the "pounced" paper with the small perforations against the car and slap the pounce pad (kind of like an eraser that's filled with dark chalk dust) against the car which

Here we have the logo, after the circle was painted black, the rim of the circle was painted in various Marblizer colors and the tape itself was pulled, leaving a reversed logo in white basecoat.

then shows the art work outline on the sides of the car in the pounce chalk.

Using the outlines left by the pounce chalk we all jump in and tape out the very intricate design. Next we tape off the circle surrounding the design before painting the area inside the circle black.

The logo area is painted with two coats of BC-25 black with normal flash time between coats. If you don't wait long enough between coats you run the risk of leaving tape marks because of solvents that are trapped. I like to see people use the touch test - before applying the next coat the paint should not feel sticky at all when you touch it with your finger.

After spraying the inside of the circle in BC 25 black (we wait 30 to 40 minutes after spraying the second coat before taping) we tape off a smaller circle and apply a variety of Marblizers for a very colorful effect. Now we can pull the tape and see the reversed house of Kolor logo in the white basecoat surrounded by black.

For painting the colors in the logo we use candy colors created with the (KK) Kandy Koncentrates and SG-100 (The SG-100 should be

After plenty of careful taping, we have the logo marked out in tape, surrounded by white basecoat.

already reduced at double the normal reduction before you add the koncentrates) We make the koncentrates in all our standard kandy colors, the code is KK. I like to mix it rich with SG - 100 so you get good intensity and then check the color on a chrome or silver stir stick. That way you can see what you've got. This covers much quicker than a regular candy. The white pearl sprayed earlier will be the base for these kandy colors.

I do the whole thing with a touch up gun, running on probably 30 psi.

Reproducing the very bright logo on the side of the car requires some very careful masking, followed by careful spraying with the touch up gun, then more masking followed by more work with the touch up gun... (for more on the logo see the color section).

Here we do the initial layout on the car, before starting on the gold and the multi colored stripes.

It's a lot of work getting the car taped off before applying the gold and everyone jumps in to help.

Here we apply the gold basecoat, which will be followed by three KK richened coats of the pagan gold kandy. By walking the length of the car and keeping the gun a uniform distance from the car (and not too far away) we are assured of even coverage.

The first thing I do will be the logo and the colors in the logo and beetle. The scarab logo is done painstakingly with the touch up gun, masking as we go. The touch up gun allows good selectivity, but some masking is necessary due to the intricacies of the design.

STRIPES ON THE NOSE

The dominant color on the car will be gold, so early in the project we tape over long panels on the sides and top of the car, leaving everything else to be painted in gold. The gold is number BC 01, solar gold. We blow off the car and wipe it down with a tack rag first, then start with one coat of adhesion promoter. The AP-01 adhesion promoter is used because the bases have gone past their "window." The adhesion promoter also guarantees adhesion of base to base paint. I apply three coats of gold after the adhesion promoter The kandy coats are next, UK 12 pagan gold kandy with some intensifier added. For the first coat the material knob is set for a lighter "bond" coat. After 3 or 4 minutes, I apply a heavier coat with the material knob backed out for more paint. The gun puts out a five inch fan five inches from the gun for both coats.

I put on a total of three coats of the kandy, one light final coat, moving fast, keeping the gun close to the car, with overlap of 75 percent. I do one with the gun at 45 degrees at the bottom and one with 50 percent going on the masking paper, that way I'm sure to get good coverage. Then one coat of UC 1, our fast setting clear (not SG-100 inter-coat clear because it cannot be used on top of catalyzed urethane).

Next the tape is pulled and we decide on the layout for the stripes that will run lengthwise on the sides and top of the car. There is enough room to run three colors, tapering in width as they go from the back to the front. The three colors are: PBC 53 lime gold in the center (chosen because we need some contrast between this gold and the pagan gold already on the car); PBC 32 tangelo blended with PBC 33 persimmon pearl; and PBC 39 hot pink blended with PBC 35 pink pearl.

I find the center of each large panel and mark that with a piece of tape. Then we layout the three areas to be painted, then pull the center tape. Next we mask off the areas prior to painting.

The outer stripes running along the side and top of the car are done next, PBC-39 hot pink Pearl, with PBC 35 pink pearl blended at the front and PBC 54 magenta pearl blended at the rear of the stripe. After three coats of the hot pink pearl the color and coverage looked too light so we add one more coat before starting to do the blends.

After the gold is dry we carefully determine the center of each panel before doing the layout and taping off the stripes.

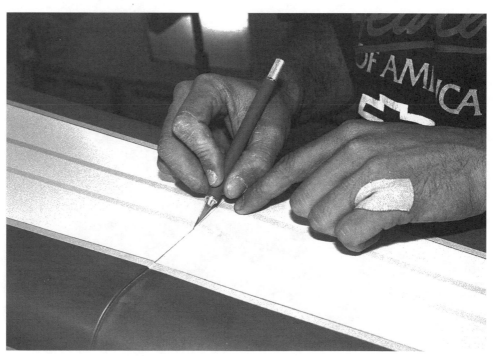

In order to keep the stripes neat where the tape crosses a body line we cut the tape with a razor blade and wrap it down into the crease.

The next stripe is done with PBC 32, tangelo pearl, with fades of persimmons and sunrise. RU 310 is the reducer used for all the pearls in this sequence (our shop temperature is 72 degrees). I put on three coats in fairly rapid succession with a standard siphon gun running on 50 PSI, keeping the gun 4 inches from the car with a restricted trigger pull. You can't wet the paint, I walk fast and put on 3 medium coats. If you wet the first coat the coverage looks uneven and then you fight it all the way

Here you see part of the stripe layout just before we put down the PBC basecoat. Note that the stripe colors will be put down over the white basecoat we applied at the start of the project.

through the next coats. When you adjust your gun do not use a full trigger pull or blotching is likely.

The blend at the front is done with PBC 31 sunset pearl while the back is done with PBC 33 persimmon,. All are reduced with RU 310, fast dry reducer. Blends are done standing in one place, with a restricted trigger pull, putting on lots of quick mist coats.

After allowing the PBCs to dry for almost 30 minutes we start in with two clearcoats using our UC-1 clear. The next step is to color sand the clear with 500 grit paper (wet) and then we can apply our pinstripes.

When the stripes are done and the tape is pulled I take a dull pocket knife and work along the paint ridges where the colors meet. It's a natural thing for the paint to climb the edge of the tape, which makes

To lay down the pinstripes we first put down 1/8 inch tape, then put quarter inch tape on either side of that, and then pull the 1/8th inch tape.

the edge thicker. You can knock most of it down with the edge of the knife. You don't really want a sharp knife that cuts into the paint, just a medium dull blade that takes off the top of the paint ridge. If you scrape the paint slightly, it's not usually a problem because you're on the SG-100 clear which was applied after each blend.

Pinstripes, done another way

The pinstriping is done by first laying down 1/8 inch masking tape with blue 1/4 inch plastic tape laid down along either side. Then the masking tape is pulled and the pinstripe can be laid down between the two pieces of plastic tape. U-9 light blue urethane striping paint is chosen for the pinstripes because it will add color to the job and complement the colors that are already there. We run over the car with a tack rag before starting on the pinstripes and signs.

The blue plastic tape must be pushed down firm. I run a rag along both pieces of tape, not my finger but a rag because it does a better job and it puts tension on the tape. The solvents in the striping paint will cause it to creep up under the tape if the tape isn't pushed down hard. We use U-00 striping reducer, our specialized reducer for brushing only. If you're going to use an airbrush then use the regular Kosmic reducers with the pinstriping urethane. Keep some of the reducer near the

We use a pinstripe brush and our pinstriping urethane, in light blue, to neaten the seam where the colors meet and to add color to the car. It's easier to pull the paint off a card as that way you can work paint up into the heel of the brush, and also because it allows you to "feel" the paint's consistency.

Even though we have a piece of tape on either side, you still have to be neat. It helps if the paint is mixed correctly so you don't leave dry spots or go back to the card for paint every two inches.

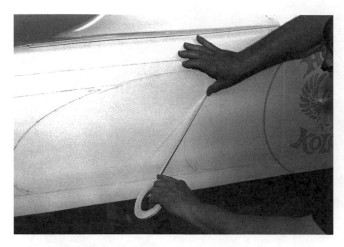

The arcs on the side of the car are taped out freehand. Note how we hold the tape with the thumb of one hand while moving the end of the tape with the other.

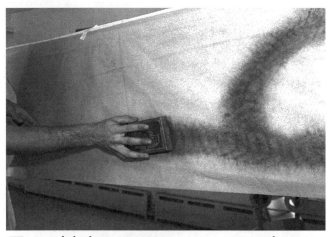

We copied the layout on tracing paper, running the pounce wheel over the outline. Then he taped the paper to the other side and used the pounce pad to transfer the outline.

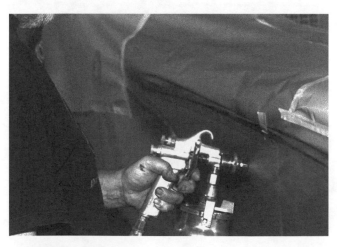

We apply the paint with a standard siphon gun, note the fine mist and how close we keep the gun to the car. Each color is blended at the front and rear and then protected by a coat of SG-100 clear.

paint and add to the "pallet" when it feels too thick. When you put your brush in the paint it should feel fairly loose with just a little tension in it.

After all the pinstriping is finished we rinse off the car and then go over it, especially the seams, with a high pressure air hose to dislodge all the remaining water or dirt.

To bury the stripes we apply another two coats of clear (UC-1) allow that to dry overnight (12 to 24 hours) and then color sand the clear with 500 grit (wet) until we can no longer feel any ridges where the stripes are. The final step is three coats of UFC-1.

MULTI COLORED ARCS OF COLOR ON THE "DOORS"

I do the initial tape out for arcs of color to the front and back of the logo circle. In order to transfer the same design and dimensions to the other side of the car, we hang masking paper on the side, then charcoal is used to outline the arcs. Then we pull the paper off the car and the pounce wheel is run along the lines marked in charcoal. After the backside of the paper is sanded to open up the holes we hang the paper on the other side of the car and run the pounce pad over the perforations.

Then we mask off the circle and shoot 3 medium coats of PBC 40 violette pearl (on the white pearl base) on the two areas closest to the logo Then we blend PBC 65 passion pearl on the outer edges for highlights and to make each colored area look like it overlaps the next.

Next the farthest forward panel is taped off and sprayed with three coats of PBC 36, true blue pearl. This will be highlighted like the inner panel, with white at the front to lighten it and green at the rear of the panel to create a teal effect. All blends are covered with at least one coat of SG-100 clear so it can be scuffed later without ruining the blend. You have to mask off everything that's less than 18 inches away, otherwise the overspray will reach it.

Now the center panel is taped off and we apply three coats of PBC 37 magic blue, highlighted at the front and the back with Magenta,

PBC 54. I like to use a 75 percent overlap when spraying the PBCs After the third coat of magic blue has flashed and the blends are done we apply one coat of SG-100 clear.

SIGNS

For the signs we have lettering done on a stencil cutter at Dick Blick Art materials in Minneapolis. These stencils are handy but they transfer glue, so you can't leave it on the car for very long, you have to get it off immediately after painting. We made a overlay for the stencil ahead of time so we can move quickly and avoid leaving the stencil on the car any longer than is absolutely necessary.

The stencil is positioned on both sides, and then one coat of BC-26 white basecoat is applied. After the white has flashed the PBC 36 blue pearl is applied with a touch up gun to the top of the lettering with PBC 40 purple pearl blended in on the bottom. Then we apply the SG-100 clearcoat, the whole procedure takes about ten minutes.

The dragster is a good example of the very nice work you can do with our House of Kolor products and a little ceativity.

The mask has adhesive on the back side, so first we stick the stencil on the car, then pull off the top layer of paper. Next we add an overlay (made up ahead of time) over the outside of the stencil, then we're ready to paint.

The signs are done by first having a mask or stencil created at a local art supply store in the size type style of our choice.

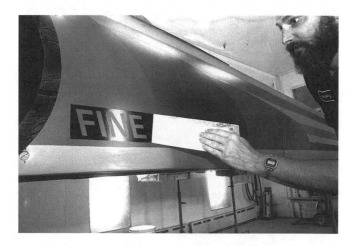

Here you see the finished product, done in two different shades of PBC over a white basecoat, and then topcoated with SG-100. It's important to work fast so there is no adhesive transfer from the backside of the stencil to the paint.

Chapter Seven

In The Shop: Custom Paint Jobs

Flames, Marblizers and Motors

This last, *In The Shop*, chapter covers three very different painting and custom painting techniques. First, people always seem to like flames and here we show how to paint a set of Harley-Davidson tanks with kandy colored flames.

Second, one of the most exciting of our new products are the Marblizer paints. By using these products you can create a marbled effect without all the hassle and hand work. By combining a given Marblizer with different colored basecoat

A successful flame job requires a good layout (done by an outside artist in this case), careful taping and skillful *application of the paint.*

and topcoats an unlimited range of effects are possible. In this chapter we show you how to use the Marblizer products to best effect.

Finally, we get a significant number of callers on our tech-line who want to know if they can use or products to paint an engine. The answer is yes, as illustrated by the last project in this chapter - the painting of a Harley-Davidson V-twin. As you look through this chapter, remember that what works for a motorcycle gas tank will work just as well on Ford fender, and that the techniques used on a V-twin work just as well on a V-8.

FLAMED TANKS

The first project in this chapter is a pair of 3-1/2 gallon Harley-Davidson Fat Bob tanks that will be painted in a multi-colored candy flame pattern. This is a good illustration not only of how to do some interesting flames, but also how to use and apply multiple kandy colors for a great custom paint job. The base for this paint is a black basecoat, already applied when we start the sequence. The flame pattern is laid out by Kevin Winter from Bloomington, Minnesota .

We start the candy flame job by spraying the base, in this case BC-02 orion silver. We use a Binks 115 (formerly called a #15) touch up gun, running on approximately 35 psi (measured at the wall) with the trigger pulled. It takes three medi-

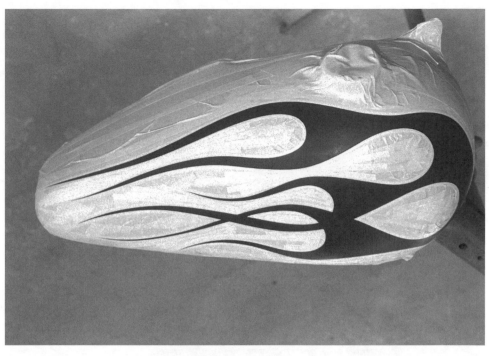

After you finish the tape-out you can really see what the flames are going to look like. It's important that all the tape be stuck down well so the paint won't creep up under the edge.

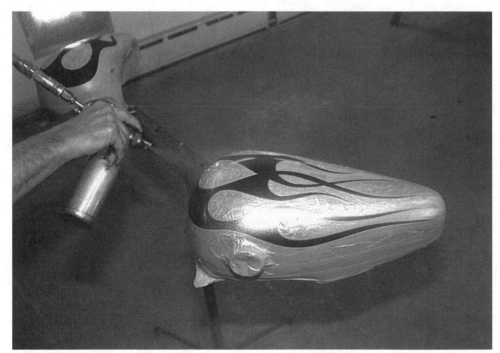

For this type of work a touch-up gun is nice because it puts out less paint and allows the painter greater control.

um coats to get the silver to cover and look good. Of note, the kandy kolors used for this sequence are KK products, or Kandy Koncentrates mixed with SG-100 clear, instead of standard urethane Kandys (UK) or acrylic lacquer kandys (K). The standard mixing guidelines for the KK products call for 16 ounces of undiluted koncentrate per one gallon of unreduced, unthinned clear (generally, the SG-100 clear is reduced 1 to 1 prior to addition of Kandy Koncentrate).

Before actually starting

Each coat of kandy makes the object darker. Though our tech sheets recommend a certain number of coats, it's a good idea to check the color against a test panel or the paint chip as you apply successive coats of paint.

The second color is applied carefully, so we get a nice blend where the two meet and not an abrupt line. (See the Color section for a look at this sequence in color). These kandy kolors are done with our Kandy Koncentrates for faster coverage.

to apply the kandy colors we do a "blend card" using a card covered with the silver base and different numbers of coats of the two colors - candy violet KK-17 and oriental blue KK-4, both mixed in SG-100. The card is done to see how the two colors are going to look at the blend point.

Though the normal instructions call for 16 ounces of concentrate per 1 gallon of unreduced, unthinned clear, we mix the koncentrate stronger in order to get the desired color in fewer coats.

The gun is adjusted

After the two basic colors are applied we tape off the areas where they overlap and apply a third color.

As we pull the tape on the overlap area you can see how we've created the impression that one lick goes over another.

117

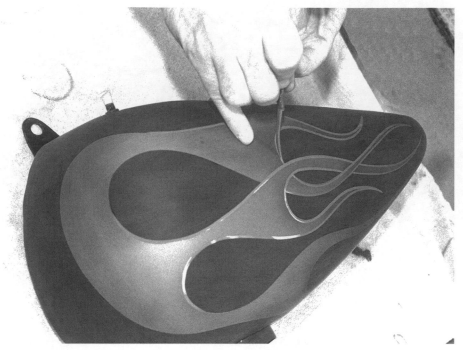

Pinstriping helps to highlight each flame lick and clean up any little mis-tapes. Here D.J. Eckel uses a natural fiber brush and our blue urethane pinstriping enamel to outline the flame job.

during the spraying as needed so the pattern will match the available area. As we narrow the pattern we are careful to also reduce the air pressure to the gun, from roughly 35 to about 20 psi as measured at the wall.

We do the violet first, at the tail of the flames, then the oriental. After each coat of kandy we check the color against the color chart. Four coats of each color are required before they match the chip in the House of Kolor color chart (because the kandies get darker with each successive coat and each painter uses the equipment a little differently, it's always a good idea to check the color against the color charts as you spray).

In order to avoid creating a dark line where the two colors overlap, we bring each successive coat of the second color a little farther into the area of the first color and use wrist action at the blend points.

After the oriental and violet are applied correctly, highlights and shadows are added in cobalt blue. This requires carefully taping off parts of the flame licks to reinforce the idea and impression that one lick goes over or under another. Highlights are done in one application, with the gun adjusted to a small round pattern. After adjusting the fan to the small pattern we further reduce the pressure to the gun and also the trigger pull (or amount of material).

Good pinstriping requires that the paint be mixed to just the right consistency By pulling the paint off the card D.J. has a chance to feel how thick the paint is before applying it to the tank.

After applying the SG-100 clear we go back into the booth and remove all the masking paper. There is always a small increase in the film thickness right where the paint meets the tape and I go over these edges with a dull knife blade. Then we take a scotch brite pad in soapy water and scuff the entire tank. This cleans up any little chips of paint on the non-flamed area and prepares the finish for the clearcoat to follow. This is also a good time to check and clean up any mis-tapes or places where the paint crept under the tape. The next step is a wipe down with a clean, dry rag, then we blow off the tanks with an air gun to remove any excess water that might be lurking on the tank or under an edge.

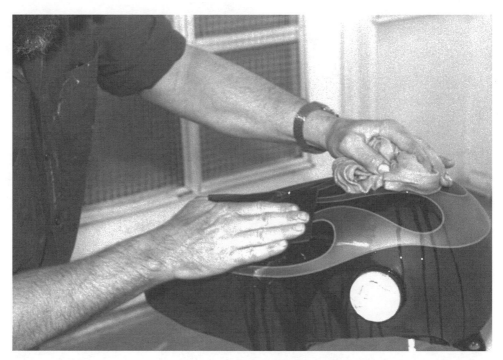

To bury the pinstriping we clear the tanks with UC-1, then wet sand with 500 grit, and apply UFC-1 as our topcoat clear.

Then we tack and apply three coats of UC-1 clear. The first coat of UC-1 is applied as a tack coat, so it won't run. After that first coat has flashed (we advise painters to use the touch test to determine flash times), two wet coats are next. After adequate drying time, the minimum is 12 hours at 70 degrees, the tank is ready for ready to be sanded and pinstriped.

To prepare the tanks for pinstriping, they are sanded with 500 grit wet paper to make sure we get a mechanical bond when we eventually clear the tanks.

PINSTRIPING
The pinstriping on this

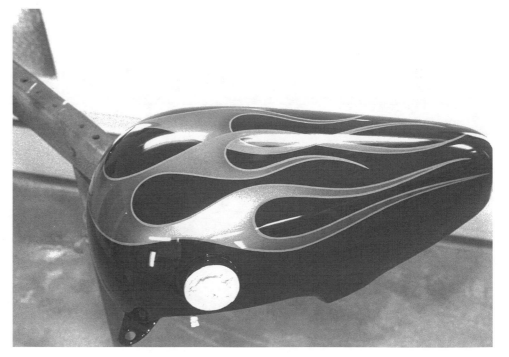

All our work of multiple clearcoats and color sanding result in tanks with a perfectly smooth surface and a great shine.

job is done by D.J. Eckel in blue using our urethane pinstriping enamel. When you take a look at the pictures, note how striping reinforces the idea that one lick goes under another.

There is always a small increase in the film thickness right where the paint meets the tape...

Take one gas tank, cover it with three coats of green basecoat, allow the last coat to flash and then get ready to apply the Marblizer of your choice.

After pinstriping the tanks go back to House of Kolor for the final clearcoats and color sanding. Before clearcoating we again wash the parts with dish soap and a grey scotch brite pad being sure to get them clean and remove any lingering finger prints.

We want to bury the pinstriping with the final clearcoats, so we use one tack coat and three wet coats, of UC-1, being careful to allow for proper flash times between coats (use touch test).

Then we allow a minimum of 12 hours at a minimum of 70 degrees for a true cure before wet sanding with 500, usually without a sanding block. We are careful not to break through into the pinstriping, because even though there are four coats of clear you can still sand through. When you can run your finger over the stripe and feel no ridge, then you're ready for the

The Marblizer Denny applies is MB-03, red-red.

final clearcoat.

We use UFC-1 as our topcoat clear, because it has a higher gloss than UC-1 and is extremely easy to buff. (But remember that the UFC-1 takes KU-500

When you can run your finger over the stripe and feel no ridge, then you're ready for the final clearcoat.

catalyst while the UC-1 takes KU-100 catalyst.)

In this case we use the UFC-1 with extra reducer as is mentioned in the tech sheet: "After color sanding re-clear using 6-8 oz of extra reducer per mixed quart of clear, the additional reducer will give you extra flowout." We apply a tack coat, wait for that to flash and then do two wet coats. Because the UFC-1 needs a longer cure time than the UC-1, we wait 24 hours before polishing. It's very important that people allow the parts to cure in a room that is at least 70 degrees.

We start the polishing sequence with the 2000 grit paper wet, and finish with the Meguiar's system of foam pads matched to the specific liquid cleaners.

USE OF MARBLIZERS

Our new marblizer products might be called artistic basecoats. By spraying these over different basecoats and topcoating

Within one minute of applying the Marblizer Denny tears off a large piece of plastic wrap and heads for the wet gas tank.

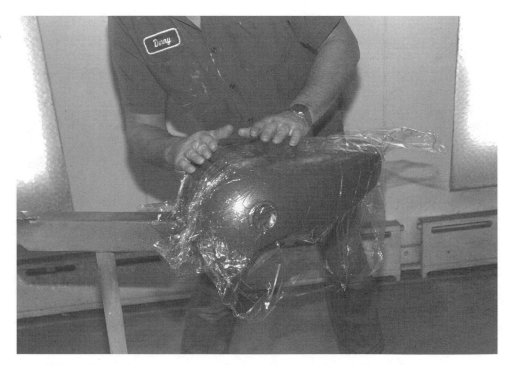

The idea is to make sure you get good contact between the plastic and the wet paint. The contact determines the pattern - some are random and some have kind of a "grain."

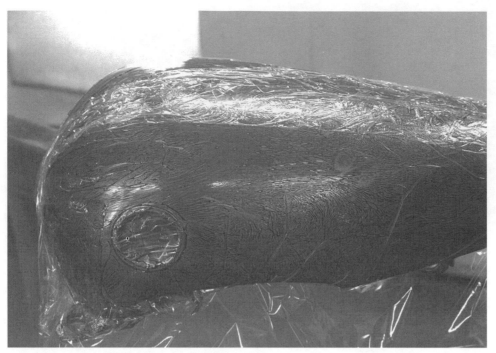

Here you can see how snug the paper is wrapped around the gas tank.

After allowing the plastic wrap to sit on the tank for about one minute Denny pulls the paper away from the tank, note that the plastic wrap is streaked with paint.

with different colors of kandy, an unlimited range of effects are possible. In this sequence we use two of our Marblizer colors to create just one of many possible effects.

First we cover the tank with one coat of Ko-seal. After waiting about 45 minutes we apply the first coat of BC-09 planet green basecoat. Denny puts on three coats with a siphon gun running at 55 psi. Denny allows flash time between coats and after allowing the third coat to flash (15 to 30 minutes) he applies the first Marblizer, MB-03, red-red

Within one minute after the Marblizer is applied, the surface is covered with plastic food wrap and then rubbed with our hands. We pull the plastic wrap right away, though you can leave it on for two minutes. After pulling the plastic wrap off we "dab" any areas of the tank that didn't get much of a marbled effect.

We let the first Marblized finish sit for 30 minutes before applying the second Marblizer, MB-02 Gold-Blue. We allow the second Marblizer to dry for another 30 minutes, then shoot a quick coat of AP-01 adhesive promoter. The AP-01 is used because the urethanes won't stick when applied over a Marblizer. You must use either SG-100 or AP-01 between the Marblizer and any urethane kandy or clear that is sprayed on top of the Marblizer.

The SG-100 is a 15 to 30 minute wait before application of the urethane (do not scuff). AP-01 is a 2 to 3 minutes wait before being topcoated with the urethane. The SG-100 works better for larger items or when art work is planned due to the fact it can be taped on.

Then we apply three coats of kandy, UK 14 Spanish gold with some KK-14 added to the mixture so it covers more quickly. The wait is five minutes between coats (use a touch test to be sure), the first two coats are medium wet sprayed with 75 percent overlap, then the third and final coat is a full wet coat sprayed with 50 percent pattern overlap.

The period of time between the last coat of kandy and the first coat of clear is usually the same as the flash time between the various kandy coats (use touch test to be sure).

Again we choose UC-1 clear as the final clearcoat. We apply two (you can use three), medium wet coats. The UC-1 must dry at least 12 hours minimum at 70 degrees. Remember that every degree under seventy slows the dry time significantly.

After drying overnight we start the color sanding. Because no other art work was done or will be done the first step is to go over the tank with 1500 grit paper (you can use 1200 to 2000 grit), wet. Ivory liquid is added to the water to prevent the paper from plugging up.

Our House of Kolor clears don't have to be polished, they dry super glossy. What we're really trying to do here is get the dust nibs out of the paint and flatten the surface. I sand any parts of the surface that have dirt in them until they're flat and show no high or low spots in the clear. For this

In areas that didn't get much of a pattern, Denny balls up the plastic wrap and "dabs" the surface while the Marblizer is still wet.

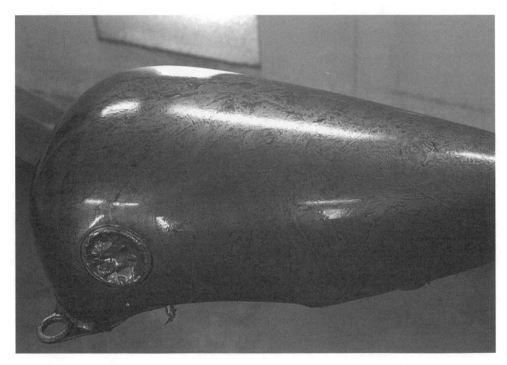

The finished Marblized pattern is a combination of the basecoat as seen through the mottled colors left by one coat of Marblizer.

After applying another coat of a different Marblizer, a kandy coat and two coats of clear, Denny starts in on the polishing. The first step is a good wet sanding with 1500 grit paper.

After smoothing out the dust nibs with the sand paper, the next step is the Meguiar's cutting pad and some number four cleaner. The next step is swirl remover and then reseal glaze, #9 is applied with a polishing pad, #7 by hand.

This is the polishing pad being used near the end of the sequence. The buffer runs at 1500 RPM (if it runs too fast it's easier to burn the paint) and should be held so the pad is pulling away from the edge so it won't catch and knock the tank off the stand.

tank we wet sanded almost the whole thing but you really only have to do the areas with dirt in the finish. Some painters do the whole surface, it's partly a matter of taste.

Once the tank has been sanded, we start the actual polishing. with the Meguiar's system. This system consists of a cutting pad and a polishing pad (both made from foam) for use on an electric polisher running at 1500 RPM.

Though a variety of compounds and glazes are available for use with this

Aluminum or cast iron, they can all be painted in much the same way you would paint a fender or gas tank.

system we start with the #4 cleaner and the cutting pad (number W-7000), working over the areas that were wet sanded (you don't need to use the cutting pad and #4 cleaner on areas that were not wet sanded).

Between steps we wipe off the tank to inspect it and to remove all of the cleaner on the tank. Next we change to the polishing pad, (W-1000L) and some #3 cleaner followed by the #9 swirl remover, changing pads with each product. The swirl remover takes out swirls left by the previous step, so you only need it on areas where you use the cutting pad.

After going over parts of the tank with the #9, we change to a fresh polishing cloth and go over the entire tank again with the #7 sealer and reseal glaze. Remember at the edges, we are careful to keep the pad spinning in such a way that it pulls away from the object and doesn't "catch" at the edge and send the object flying or put a burn spot in the paint.

HOW TO PAINT ENGINES

Painting an engine, whether it's a V-twin or a V-eight, isn't difficult. Aluminum or cast iron, they can all be painted in much the same way you would paint a fender or gas tank. And if you can paint an engine then you can obviously paint a

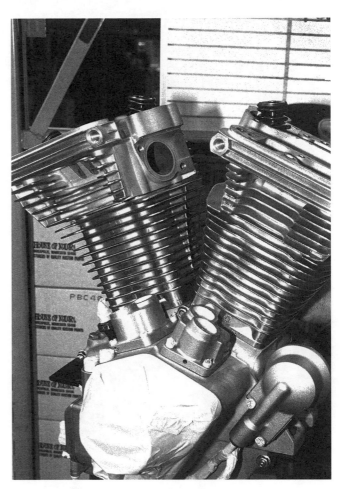

Masking off the engine is one of the most time consuming parts of the operation - especially for an air-cooled V-twin. Here Mike Marquart's engine is part way though the masking operation.

transmission in the same way.

The most important thing is to get everything clean, really clean. And you have to be sure to use a good primer. Of course, any primer you use should be a catalyzed two-part product like our KP-2. Because engines live in such a harsh environment with heat and chemicals, no lacquer paints should be used. Only catalyzed urethanes are good enough to topcoat your automotive or motorcycle engine.

The engine seen here is a late model V-twin from Mike Marquart's Harley-Davidson. The paint job is being done following a complete rebuild. While the engine was apart Mike had the fins polished (on the aluminum cylinders) to a high luster, so the first thing to do is clean the

Because the edges of the fins have been polished, Mike tapes off each edge. He applies quarter inch tape and then trims it to size with an X-acto knife.

freshly painted engine). It's a very time consuming operation but well worth the effort in the end. If the engine is a V-eight, you still have to mask off all the port openings, the valve train and so on.

After taping we apply one medium coat of KP-2. This way the primer can be topcoated in 60 to 90 minutes and no sealer is required.

Note: Because no sealer will be used on this engine I like to do extra straining of the primer with a clean-wipe, so there are no contaminants that might cause a bump - because sealers are not sanded after application.

It's very important to get paint applied from all angles, to get at all the areas that are masked by fins and such. A second coat, done right after the first, can be used to minimize the roughness seen on some of castings.

The black is UB 4, (I recommend the UB 4

No sealer will be used on this engine, so the primer will be uses as the sealer. It's important to strain the primer in situations like this so there are no lumps in it - because you're not going to sand this primer.

engine, being sure that all the polishing rouge is cleaned away. Dish detergent and hot water is a good way to clean the parts before assembly. In fact, some people put the engine parts in the dishwasher at home. Next comes a good washing with some final wash or solvent that will not leave any residue behind. We use acetone for cleaning off the oily fingerprints but you could use a similar solvent that leaves no residue behind.

TAPING

Taping off the areas that you don't want painted is one of the most time consuming parts of this operation, especially for a motorcycle engine. Mike Marquart used quarter inch tape which he stretched across the fins and then cut to fit with an X-acto knife (this is easier than polishing off the paint later and making a mess all over your

Painting engines is hard, the paint seems to want to blow back at you. You have to apply the paint from different angles so you're sure to get coverage between all those fins.

instead of UFB for engines) applied lightly for the first coat. I use a little accelerator, (not over 16 drops per mixed quart) so it will dry quicker and we can put on three coats in rapid succession.

For this job I use a siphon style touch up gun, running on 35 to 45 psi with the trigger pulled. It's really hard to paint these engines, it's like the

part primer, skip the sealer and be sure everything is squeaky clean before you start.

Painting an engine is not magic, just another case of using the right materials…

paint wants to blow back at you as you move the gun over the surfaces. You have to be careful to get good coverage over the entire engine.

After allowing the paint to set up and dry, the tape is pulled (sooner rather than later so the tape won't pull the paint with it) polished areas like fins can be cleaned of any overspray with a little acetone or lacquer thinner on a rag, being careful not to get any on the finish paint.

The three coats were applied in rapid succession. as soon as one coat was tacky (or does not string to the finger) we went in with the next coat.

Painting an engine is not magic, just another case of using the right materials for the job and following the correct procedures for those products. Use catalyzed urethanes over a two-

It's a lot of work carefully taping off all those fins, but worth it in the end. Like any other painting operation, it's the preparation of the engine that takes most of the time. For a finished look at this engine turn to the color section.

Sources

House of Kolor
2521 - 27th Avenue South
Minneapolis, MN 55406

House of Kolor Tech Line:
(612) 729-1044

D.J. Eckel Sign and Striping Company
3500 Bloomington Avenue South
Minneapolis MN 55407
(612) 721-3456

Kirby's Custom Paint
Precision Paint Removers
2415 W Industrial Boulevard - Bay 1
Long Lake MN 55356
(612) 476 4545

Morgan Manufacturing
521 Second Street
Petaluma, CA 95942
(707) 763-6848